THE WINDOWS COMMAND LINE BEGINNER'S GUIDE - SECOND EDITION

JONATHAN MOELLER

DESCRIPTION

The Windows Command Line Beginner's Guide gives users new to the Windows command line an overview of the Command Prompt, from simple tasks to network configuration.

In the Guide, you'll learn how to:

-Manage the Command Prompt.

-Copy & paste from the Windows Command Prompt.

-Create batch files.

-Remotely manage Windows machines from the command line.

-Manage disks, partitions, and volumes.

-Set an IP address and configure other network settings.

-Set and manage NTFS and file sharing permissions.

-Customize and modify the Command Prompt.

-Create and manage file shares.

-Copy, move, and delete files and directories from the command line.

-Manage processes from the command line.

-And many other topics.

LEGAL

INTRODUCTION

Welcome to "The Windows Command Line Beginner's Guide!" If you're reading this book, you have the opportunity to benefit from the power and flexibility of the Windows command line. Novice users can use the Windows command prompt to make repetitive tasks far quicker and easier, while advanced users can modify network settings, alter system configurations, and even use the command line to remotely control distant Windows machines.

What Is The Windows Command Line?

Generally, the "Windows command line" refers to a program called the "Command Prompt", or CMD.EXE, that has been included with every version of Windows since Windows 2000. CMD.EXE is Windows's built-in commander interpreter. If you're not familiar with the term, a "command interpreter" is a program that takes lines of text entered by the computer operator (i.e, you) and converts them into commands the computer can understand. A command prompt is commonly referred to as a command-line interface or a CLI.

With the Windows Command Prompt, you can open up a

command-line window on your Windows system. Within Command Prompt's window, you can use the full range of command-line utilities included with the system. You can even open multiple command-line windows, if you want to run more than one command at once.

Of course, nowadays most computers use a graphical user interface (abbreviated GUI), with a mouse pointer, windows, scroll bars, icons, and other graphical metaphors instead of text commands. In fact, a great majority of computer users have never even used a command-line interface. Windows is famous for its graphical interface – even its name, "Windows", refers to the graphical windows drawn on the screen of a Windows desktop or server computer. It might seem surprising that an operating system that relies upon a GUI like Windows still includes something as apparently archaic as a command-line interface.

However, Windows owes its existence to an older and simpler operating system – Microsoft Disk Operating System, MS-DOS, or as it is more commonly known, DOS. DOS originated during the early days of the personal computer revolution in the late 1970s and the early 1980s. As the personal computer market grew, IBM, a major manufacturer of high-powered mainframe computers, decided to market its own personal computer. Rather than designing specific IBM components for its personal computer, IBM decided to use off-the-shelf parts, and bought the operating system – specifically, MS-DOS, from a small Seattle company called Microsoft. IBM let Microsoft keep the rights to DOS, figuring that the real value of a personal computer lay in the hardware, not the software.

(IBM would come to regret this decision.)

As the IBM PC, and later IBM PC compatibles, took off, the PC platform faced competition from Apple's Macintosh computer. The Macintosh relied on a GUI, which was far more user-friendly than the white text interface and cryptic error messages of the early versions of DOS. Recognizing the danger, Microsoft and IBM began joint work on a next-generation 32-bit graphical operating system called OS/2. Eventually Microsoft and IBM broke their alliance, leaving IBM with sole control over OS/2.

Microsoft pursued its own line of graphical operating systems, which it named "Windows." The early versions of Windows were a graphical shell riding upon DOS – the user typed "win" at the command line to launch the Windows interface. The early versions of Windows – 3.0, 3.1, and 3.11, all were graphical interfaces on top of the old DOS operating system. Even the Windows 9x line of operating systems – 95, 98, and Millennium Edition – ran on top of DOS.

However, Microsoft had created a 32-bit version of Windows called Windows NT (the "NT" stood for "new technology") to compete with IBM's OS/2. Unlike the Windows 9x line of operating systems, NT was a truly graphical operating system – the GUI did not run on top of DOS. With the release of Windows XP in 2001, Microsoft's consumer-based line of operating systems merged with the NT line of operating systems (Windows XP was technically Windows NT 5.1), and the days of DOS had come to an end.

However, Windows XP still kept the command-line interface in the form of the Command Prompt application. Windows Vista and Windows 7 & 8 followed suit, as did Microsoft's line of server operating systems – Windows Server 2003, Windows Server 2003 R2, Windows Server 2008, Windows Server 2008 R2, and Windows Server 2012. DOS is history, but thanks to the Command Prompt application, you can still use the old DOS commands on a modern Windows system.

Why Learn The Command Line?

You might wonder why you would want to learn the command line, since Windows comes with a perfectly fine graphical user interface. Just because Windows comes with the command line doesn't mean you have to run it, after all. And what possible use could you get out of it?

For one, the command line permits you to perform numerous repetitive and tedious computing tasks far more quickly. For example, let's say you need to copy a large number of JPEG image files out of your Pictures folder and onto your flash drive (which Windows has assigned the letter J:). Your JPEGS are named for the month and day they were taken – August01.JPEG, March01.JPEG, and so forth. Specifically, let's say that you need to copy every JPEG taken in the month of August to your flash drive.

To copy the files, you could drag-and-drop every single one of the files, or CTRL-click each of the files, and then drag them to your flash drive. Either way, it would take a great deal of bother and hassle.

Or you could simply type this command at the Command Prompt:

COPY c:\username\pictures\August*.JPEG J:

This command will copy every JPEG file beginning with "August" in your Pictures folder to your flash drive. Needless to say, this is vastly more efficient than dragging and dropping, copying & pasting, or CTRL-clicking from the GUI.

Information technology professionals, such as help desk technicians and network administrators, have an even greater motivation to learn the command line. Everything in Windows can be done through the GUI. However, many tasks can be performed far more efficiently at the Command Prompt. In particular, it is easier to do numerous network tasks from the command line than through the GUI. For example, finding your IP address on a Windows 7 desktop system takes five different mouse clicks and four separate dialog boxes. Finding your computer's IP address from the Command Prompt takes one brief command.

And on a Windows system, many network diagnostic tools are available only through the command line. If your system loses its network connection, the graphical tools aren't terribly helpful. The command line utilities are far more efficient at discovering the root of the problem, if you know how to use them properly.

Finally, the command line offers the advantage of automation. An IT professional will often find himself dealing with repetitive and tedious tasks. Using the Command Prompt, is possible to create simple scripts called "batch files" to deal with these boring jobs. Instead of typing the same sequence of commands over and over again, or wading through graphical menu after graphical menu, a well-written batch file can handle these tasks with a single typed command.

The Purpose Of This Book

The purpose of this book is to provide a basic introduction to using the Windows Command Prompt. It's not intended as an exhaustive or comprehensive overview, but as an introduction to the topic - enough to get you started, and comfortable enough to start experimenting on your own. (Feel free to jump around if a particular topic interests you more than the others.) We can divide this book into three parts:

-Part I: Command line basics and file management basics.

-Part II: Networking.

-Part III: Advanced tasks - disk management, remote management, batch files, and others.

Why I Wrote This Book

I began writing about computers and technology almost by accident. I started my writing career as a writer of fantasy fiction (my sword-and-sorcery novels are now available in all major eBook formats), and like every good fantasy writer, I had a blog that tended to pull down only thirty or forty hits a month. One day I happened to write about a problem I had with a file server, and the next day I was surprised to see nearly sixty hits come in via Google searches for that same problem. From there it was a short step to blogging regularly about technology (and turning a profit via web ads), and then when the eBook revolution struck, to writing short eBooks on technical topics.

I decided to write this book because an entire generation of computer users, those born after 1990 or so, have no experience of using a command-line interface. Many high school and college students only began using computers after GUIs became dominant, and therefore have no idea how to use the Command Prompt, or are even aware that it exists. It is my hope that this book will help anyone to learn to use the Windows command-line interface, and show them ways to make their computer more efficient and useful.

A Note About Windows Versions

All the commands discussed in this book will work on Windows 7, Windows 8, Windows 8.1, Windows 10, Windows Server 2008, Windows Server 2008 R2, Windows Server 2012, and Windows Server 2012 R2. Most of them will work on Windows Vista, Windows Server 2003 R2, and Windows Server 2003. Many of the commands will work on older versions of Windows, but the older the version of Windows, the less likely the commands will work. In particular, many of the network commands used in the modern versions of Windows will not work on the older Windows 9x family of operating systems.

Errata

I have done my best to make sure that all the information in this book is accurate and timely, and tested every command and procedure described in the following chapters. However, I am only mortal, and undoubtedly I have made mistakes. If you notice any errors, you can email me at jmcontact @ jonathanmoeller.com to let me know. The advantage of eBooks over paper books is that eBooks are vastly easier to update and revise, and I can quickly introduce a revised and updated version to correct any mistakes. (Another advantage of ebooks over paper books is that you can have it open on your computer screen as you try out the commands, rather than having to look down at a paper book on your desk.)

Notes On The Second Edition

This book has sold far better than I anticipated. That, combined with changes in Windows 8. Windows 8.1, and Windows 10 made it necessary to create a second edition. In this edition, I have added sections dealing with the Command Prompt in these versions of Windows. I have also added a new chapter describing how to perform task management from the command line itself, and a new section in Chapter 1 describing how to change the size of the Command Prompt window.

1

COMMAND LINE BASICS

B y default, Windows boots into a graphical interface. In fact, if Windows boots into something other than the default graphical interface, you can safely assume that something has gone wrong with your system (or that you have booted into one of the versions of Safe Mode). How, then, to launch the Command Prompt from the GUI?

In this chapter, we'll discuss how to launch the Command Prompt, and a few basics about using the Windows command line. We'll also talk about command history, how to copy and paste, the case sensitivity of the Command Prompt, and a few other useful topics.

Launching The Command Line

You can launch the Command Prompt like any other Windows application. To do so, go to the Start Menu, and then to the Accessories folder. Inside the Accessories folder, you'll see the icon for the Command Prompt – it will look like a little black square with white text in it. Click on that icon, and the Command Prompt window will launch.

You can also launch the Command Prompt using the Start Menu Search feature that has been included with every version of Windows since Vista launched in late 2006. When you click on the Start Menu button, you'll see a Search field at the bottom of the left-hand pane in the Start Menu. In that field, type "command", and the Command Prompt should appear as the top hit. To find it even faster, just type "cmd" (the Command Prompt's real name is CMD.EXE, after all), and again the Command Prompt should be the top hit.

There is an even faster method of launching the Command Prompt. Most computers produced in the last ten years include the "Windows key", which is usually between the CTRL and ALT keys on the left side of the keyboard (desktop USB keyboards generally include a second Windows key between the right CTRL and ALT keys). If you hit the Windows key and the R key simultaneously, this will bring up the Run box. If you type the name of a program or file into the Run box, Windows will launch or open it for you. You can launch the Command prompt by simply typing "cmd" into the Run window and hitting ENTER or clicking OK.

LAUNCHING THE COMMAND LINE FROM WINDOWS 8, 8.1, & 10

IF YOU HAVE USED Windows 8, you know that the new user interface (commonly called the "Modern Style UI") in Windows 8 is very different from the traditional Windows environment. Fortunately, launching the Command Prompt from Windows 8 is quite simple, and Windows 8 offers options for launching the Command Prompt that previous versions of Windows do not possess.

To launch the Command Prompt in Windows 8, tap the WINDOWS key to summon the Start Screen. Once the Start Screen appears, you can use its integrated search function to find the Command Prompt by typing "cmd." (There's no actual "search box" –

just start typing at the Start Screen, and Windows 8 will begin searching for you.) Once you type "cmd", the tile for Command Prompt will appear. Click on it, and you will be taken from the Start Screen to the Desktop, which will have an open Command Prompt window.

Windows 8 and up also include File Explorer, an improved version of the Windows Explorer shell. File Explorer offers the ability to launch a Command Prompt window within the folder you are currently viewing. To do so, click on the File tab in the upper left-hand corner of the File Explorer window, and then select "Open Command Prompt" from the menu. You will have the option to choose between launching a Command Prompt window as a standard user or as a administrative user. (We'll discuss that, and User Account Control, more later in this chapter.)

For more information about Windows 8 in general, I suggest my book The Windows 8 Beginner's Guide.

Running The Command Line As An Administrator

From time to time you might get in an error message in the Command Prompt that "this operation requires elevation" or that "this command must be run as an administrator." What does that mean?

Windows Vista, Windows 7, Windows Server 2008 / 2008 R2, and Windows Server 2012 and up use a security technology called "User Account Control." User Account Control (UAC) is a method of locking down user accounts in order to protect Windows systems from viruses, Trojans, and other forms of malware. Basically, a Windows system has two kinds of user accounts – administrative user accounts, which can install programs and alter system settings, and standard user accounts, which can run programs, but can't install software or alter settings. In Windows XP, most people used local administrator accounts, which made it easy for malware to install itself undetected in the background.

UAC provides a level of protection against that kind of attack.

Under UAC, all accounts, even administrator accounts, run as normal accounts. When you do something that requires administrative privileges, such as installing a program, or trying to change a system setting, the screen freezes and the UAC prompt appears. For administrative users, the UAC prompt reads "Do you want to allow the following program to make changes to this computer?" followed by buttons for Yes or No. Standard users are prompted to enter an administrative username and password to continue.

Because of this, Command Prompt usually opens with the permissions of a standard user, even when you launch it from an administrator's account. This means you won't be able to use Command Prompt to launch any commands that alter the system or install programs. To do so, you will need to run Command Prompt as an administrator.

Fortunately, running any program as an administrator within Windows is easy. Simply right-click on the icon for Command Prompt and select "Run as administrator" from the context menu that appears (it will have the multicolored shield icon of the UAC prompt next to it). If you're running within an administrator account, you need only click Yes to continue; if you're using a standard user account, you'll need to enter an administrator's username and password. Once Command Prompt opens as an administrator, the program's title bar will change from "Command Prompt" to "Administrator", and you can now launch commands that will affect system settings.

Making The Command Prompt Window Larger

By default, the Command Prompt window is not very large. Even if you maximize it, the window will not take up more than a third of your screen or so. If you want a larger window, right-click on the Command Prompt window's title bar, and select Properties. When the Properties window opens up, click on the Layout Tab.

The Layout tab lets you control the size of your Command Prompt window. The easiest way to do so is to adjust the numbers in the Window Size category. By adjusting the Height and the Width numbers, you can make the Command Prompt window as small or as large as you like. Once you have finished, click on the OK button, and the size of the Command Prompt window will change to your specifications.

(Personally, I find that a small window is more useful, since that allows you to read directions off a web page or an ebook while you work.)

Tab Completion

Back in the old days of DOS, filenames and directory names were limited to only eight characters, with no spaces, and another three characters to denote the file extension (used by the operating system to determine what program to use to open the file - a TXT extension means that the file is a text file, for example). These were called 8.3 filenames, and as you can imagine, the limitation led to some creative and cryptic naming of documents. A file might have a name like "THSREV2.DOC", and it would take a creative thinker indeed to realize that the file name refers to the second revision of the author's senior thesis.

All modern versions of Windows support "long file names", which means you can have file names up to 255 characters long. And the file names can even include spaces! So instead of "THSREV2.DOC", the author could name his file "Second Revision of Senior Thesis.DOC" with room to spare.

However, short file names have one advantage - they're easier to type at the command line. Typing "THSREV2.DOC" as the Command Prompt is easy, but typing "Second Revision of Senior Thesis.DOC" takes rather longer.

This is where tab completion comes in handy.

Type the first part of a file name, hit TAB, and Command Prompt will take its best stab at filling out the rest of the file's name for you. For instance, let's say you wanted to use the DEL command to delete a file named test.txt located at C:\users\camalas\documents\test.txt. You could type out the entire file name and path.

Or you could type the command and the first part of the path:

DEL C:\us

Hit the TAB key, and the command will look like this:

DEL C:\Users

Add an additional backlash and the letter C, hit the TAB key, and Command Prompt will fill out the next step in the path:

DEL C:\Users\camalas

Using tab completion, you can fill out the entire file location bit by bit, which is far quicker than typing out the entire path.

What happens if two files in the same directory have similar names, like Caina1.doc and Caina2.doc? In that case, tab completion will sort through the files in alphabetical order. Say you typed this command and then hit the TAB key:

DEL Caina

The Command Prompt would first produce this:

DEL Caina1.doc

But if you hit the TAB key for a second time, it would switch to this:

DEL Caina2.doc

With tab completion, you can type long filenames far quicker than you could otherwise.

Filenames With Spaces

In the DOS era, you couldn't have filenames or directory names with spaces. But as we've mentioned, in modern versions of Windows, you can have filenames up to 255 characters long, including spaces. In fact, you can have any characters you want in a filename, except for a forward slash (/), a backslash (\), a colon (:), an asterisk (*), a less than sign (<), a greater than sign (>), and a pipe (|). The reason is that many of these characters serve as filename wildcards and command redirection characters, which we shall discuss in greater detail in Chapter 6.

But back to filenames with spaces. The Mac OS X and the Linux command line require you to denote spaces in file names with slashes or quotation marks, since otherwise their command-line interpreters will not parse the spaces properly. The Windows Command Prompt, however, can handle spaces just fine. For instance, if you want to change to the Program Files directory, you would simply type this command:

CD \Program Files

And with tab completion, you can quickly fill out "Program Files" without having to type the entire name.

There are certain circumstances, such as batch files, where using the full name with spaces is undesirable. For every long file name, Windows also generates a hidden 8.3 filename, since certain applications and situations require a shorter file name. We'll discuss how to find those short 8.3 filenames when we discuss the DIR command in detail in Chapter 4.

Copying And Pasting

Many Command Prompt commands are long and complicated. Even with tab completion, typing them out can be a chore. Copying and pasting complex commands into the Command Prompt would make things easier - both the Mac OS X and Linux terminal applications include Edit menus in their menu bars that allow users to paste commands into the prompt and copy the output of the commands. Why not do the same with Windows?

Unfortunately, this is one area where the Windows Command Prompt falls behind the command-line applications of competing operating system. The Command Prompt does not have the typical Windows menu bar, which means it has neither the Edit menu nor the Copy and Paste items. To make matters worse, the standard CTRL+C shortcut for Copy and the CTRL+V shortcut for Paste do not work in Command Prompt.

That said, it is possible to copy text from and paste text into the Command Prompt. It just takes a little more work than most other

Windows applications. We'll first discuss how to paste items into the Command Prompt, and then how to copy text from the prompt.

The Command Prompt doesn't have the usual Windows menu bar, but it does have a menu of its own in the upper-left hand corner of the title bar, indicated by the small Command Prompt icon. Left-click on this icon to summon the Command Prompt menu, and you'll see an option for Edit about two-thirds of the way down. Move your mouse pointer over that, and the menu will expand to show the usual Edit options, including Paste, along with a few others. Click on Paste, and any text currently on your clipboard (such as a copied command) will be pasted into Command Prompt.

Copying from the Command Prompt is a bit trickier. By default, you can't highlight text within the Command Prompt window. To highlight text, go to the Command Prompt menu, to the Edit category, and then click Mark. You'll now be able to highlight text within the Command Prompt windows. Next, go back to the menu, to Edit, and select Copy – the highlighted text will be copied to your clipboard. (While text is highlighted, you can also use the Enter key to copy.) You can then Paste it into the application of your choice – this is especially useful when you're getting an error message, and you want to email it to a technician or post it to a forum.

Copying text in this way is rather cumbersome. There is a way to speed it up. If you right-click on Command Prompt's title bar and click on Properties, this will take you to the Properties dialog box. Most of the Properties dialog box's tabs let you control the shape, color, and font size of the Command Prompt. But under the options tab, there is a check box labeled "Insert Mode." If you check that, it will be as if the Mark option is turned on in Command Prompt all the time – you can highlight text simply by left-clicking and dragging the mouse cursor over it, rather than going to the menu, selecting Edit, and then clicking on Mark every time you want to copy some text.

Finding Text

During a long Command Prompt session, the window tends to fill up with a lot of text – command outputs, directory listings, and so forth. If you want to find a particular item, you can scroll back up through the session, but that can take a long time. The Command Prompt's menu includes a Find item, which lets you search the output of your commands for a particular word or phrase.

To use it, go to the Command Prompt menu in the upper-left hand corner, select the Edit item, and then click on Find. This will bring up a Find box, similar to the Find box in other Microsoft applications like Notepad and WordPad. Type the word or term you want to find into the search box and hit Find Next, and Command Prompt will find the term in the output of your session. Keep hitting Find Next to find additional instances of the term. You can also use the radio buttons under Direction to choose whether Command Prompt will search your term from the top of the screen down or from the bottom of the screen upward.

Clearing The Screen

During a busy Command Prompt session, the window will fill up with quite a bit of text. This can get rather cluttered, so you might want to clear the window entirely. Simply type this command at the prompt:

CLS

And your Command Prompt window will be cleared.

Note that all the text in the windows is gone forever after you use the CLS command, so if you want to copy and paste anything out the window, do so before using the cls command.

Command History

As you use the Command Prompt, you might find yourself reusing the same commands, or similar commands, over and over again. You could of course retype them, but Command Prompt offers a feature called command history that makes retyping the commands unnecessary. Command history remembers the last fifty commands you type, and you can recall them to the prompt by pressing the UP arrow key on your keyboard. Keep pressing UP to scroll through the list of commands until you find the one you need. If you go too far into the list, you can use the DOWN arrow key to scroll backwards through the commands.

If command history doesn't remember enough commands for your liking, you can adjust the number by right-clicking on Command Prompt's title bar and selecting Properties. Under the Options tab, there is a heading for Command History, and you can increase and decrease the buffer size for stored commands there.

Case Sensitivty

If you've ever used the command line for Mac OS X or Linux, you know that their command line applications are case sensitive. That means their command interpreters distinguish between uppercase and lowercase letters. For instance, a Linux command line would view COPY, Copy, and copy as three separate commands. Likewise, a Linux command line would view Report.doc, REPORT.doc, and report.doc as three separate files.

Unlike Linux or Mac OS X, the Windows Command Prompt is not case sensitive, and does not distinguish between commands or filenames based up the case of the letters in the file name. To return to the previous example, the Command Prompt will interpret COPY, Copy, and copy as the same thing - every one of these will launch the copy command. In the same vein, Command Prompt will view Report.doc, REPORT.doc, and report.doc as the same file - it will not distinguish filenames based on the case of the letters in the filename.

This generally makes the Windows Command Prompt easier to use than the Mac OS X or Linux terminals, especially for new users.

For the sake of readability in this book, all commands will be typed in ALL CAPS, but it makes absolutely no difference whether you type the commands in uppercase, lowercase, or a mix of the two.

Executable Files

There are limitations to the kind of files you can open and programs you can launch from the Windows Command Prompt. You can open documents and image files from the Command Prompt - if you type the file name and hit enter, Windows will attempt to open the document using the default program for opening that type of file. If you type a filename and Command Prompt doesn't recognize it, you'll get this error message:

FILENAME is not recognized as an internal or external command, operable program or batch file.

(FILENAME, of course, is whatever you typed that Command Prompt doesn't recognize.)

So what does Command Prompt mean by "internal or external command, operable program, or batch file?" There are three different kinds of commands you can actually execute from the Command Prompt: COM files, EXE files, and BAT files. (There are actually more than three, but most people will only encounter these three kinds.)

A COM file is generally a "command" file, and refers to the commands included with Windows for use in Command Prompt. A large percentage of the commands we'll discuss in this book are actually COM files tucked away somewhere in your hard drive's \Windows directory. Occasionally commercial programs have a COM extension, but not very often.

Most commercial programs, and some Windows programs, are EXE files - executable files. Almost all programs written nowadays are stored in EXE files. Many of Windows's graphical applications have a file extension of EXE. You can run some EXE files from the Command Prompt, but many EXE files can only be run in the graphical environment of Windows.

The final kind of executable file is a BAT file, a batch file. Batch files are different from COM and EXE files. Both COM and EXE files are binary files, and if you opened them with a text editor like Notepad, you would see only gibberish. Batch files, by contrast, are text files containing a list of commands. When you run a batch file from Command Prompt, it executes the commands in the batch file, one by one.

We'll discuss batch files more in Chapter 13.

Getting Help

Each command offers its own array of switches and options, and keeping track of them all can prove quite a challenge. Fortunately, every command supports the /? switch. Type any command with the /? switch appended, and Command Prompt will list the available options for the command. For example:

XCOPY /?

This will list all the options available for the XCOPY command.

DRIVE LETTERS AND THE FILE SYSTEM

I f you've ever opened My Computer on Windows XP or Computer on Windows Vista and up, right away you've seen a large number of drives. Some of them might have been your computer's internal hard drives and optical drives. Others might have belonged to USB drives, like external hard drives or flash drives. Still others might have belonged to your computer's built-in media card reader, if your system has one. And if you have an old computer, you might even still have a letter assigned to a floppy drive, though floppy drives are becoming rarer and rarer. (Thankfully, in my opinion-floppy drives are slow and unreliable, and a $10 four gigabyte flash drive can hold the contents of roughly 1,500 three-and-a-half inch floppy disks.)

Before you can use the Command Prompt effectively, you need to understand how drive letters work, and how the Windows file system is laid out. We'll address both these topics in this chapter.

Drive Letters

In the Windows operating system, every physical drive (or logical partition on a physical drive – more on those in Chapter 9) is assigned a drive letter. For instance, your first hard drive might receive the letter C, your first optical drive the letter D, and so forth. This is different from Mac OS X and Linux, where additional drives generally show up as subfolders on the hard drive – usually in the /media or the /Volumes folder (a USB flash drive with a volume label of STORAGE would show up with a drive letter on a Windows system, but as the /Volumes/STORAGE directory on a Mac).

Why use drive letters? They provide a convenient way of finding which disk is holding a particular file. If you know that the full path to a file named Book.doc is C:\Storage\Book.doc file, then you know that the file is on the C drive, which is probably the first hard drive on your system.

Any drive can be assigned any letter. However, by tradition and convention (and in some cases technical requirements) certain letters usually get assigned to certain kinds of drives. The letters A and B are rarely used on modern Windows systems – in older DOS computers, the letters A and B were reserved for the first and second floppy drives in the system.

The letter C is almost always assigned to the first hard drive (or hard drive partition) in a system, generally the partition or hard drive where Windows is installed. On a modern computer, you can install Windows on any hard drive with any letter. However, it is usually best to install Windows on C, since many older (and badly-written) programs expect to find Windows on the C drive, and refuse to run if Windows is installed on any other drive letter.

The letter D, traditionally, is assigned to the first optical drive in the computer – a CD-ROM, DVD-ROM, CD-RW, or DVD-RW drive (or a drive that combines all four functions, as most modern drives do). However, on many modern laptops and desktops, the D drive is assigned to a recovery partition on the hard drive, which contains the files necessary to reinstall Windows from scratch in case of operating system corruption or irreparable virus damage. (Computer manufacturers started doing this to save on the cost of including a recovery DVD with the system.) If your system has a recovery partition on D, then your first optical drive will receive the letter of E.

After D and E, there is no generally agreed convention for which devices get which letters. As you add drives to your system, whether internal hard drives or removable USB flash drives and hard drives, Windows will assign them the next available letter. If you want a device to have a different letter, you can reassign the letter either using the Disk Management snap-in in the Computer Management console, or using the DISKPART command-line utility (more on DISKPART in Chapter 9).

The Path

As you work with the Command Prompt, you might notice that in order to run an executable file you need to either change to the directory containing a file, or type its full path at the prompt. However, for many of the built-in Windows commands, you can type the command in any directory, and Command Prompt will run it. Why is that?

This is something called the system path, or generally just the path, that Command Prompt uses to find commands. Basically, the path consists of a few directories set apart by Windows for storing commands. If you type a command at the prompt, Command Prompt searches the directories in the path for the command. If it doesn't find the command in the path, it then checks the current directory. And if it doesn't find the command there, it comes back with the usual error message:

FILENAME is not recognized as an internal or external command, operable program or batch file.

If you want to find out what your system's path is, simply type the PATH command at the prompt:

PATH

The results will generally look something like this:

C:\Windows\system32;C:\Windows;C:\Windows\System32\Wbem

Command Prompt will search these three directories for commands. There might be other directories in your system's path – installed programs sometimes add their directories to the path. You can also add directories to the path using the PATH command, though it's best to do so sparingly. If you add too many commands to the path, Command Prompt will search them all to find a command, which can slow down system performance.

Network Drives

From the days of Windows for Workgroups in the early 1990s, Windows has offered strong support for file sharing – accessing files stored in a shared folder on a remote server. It is possible to connect file shares to your computer and assign them a drive letter – a process called "drive mapping" or "mapping a network drive." Once a shared folder has been mapped to your computer as a network drive, you can use it like any other kind of drive, copying files to and from it (though that may depend on your permissions to the shared folder). We'll discuss network drives more in Chapter 10.

The Windows File System

We've been talking about "directories", but what do we mean by that term?

If you look at the root of your C drive through Windows Explorer, you'll see a number of different folder icons. A "directory" is a virtual folder that allows you to sort and organize your files into different containers, so everything isn't messily stored in just one folder. (In fact, in earlier versions of Windows, if you had too many items in your hard drive's root directory, Windows mistakenly assumed that your hard drive had filled up!)

You could put additional directories inside directories – these directories within directories are called "subdirectories." You can put additional subdirectories within those subdirectories, as many as you wish. If you think of the root directory of your hard drive (represented by the \ character) as the trunk of a tree, then the directories and their subdirectories are branches off the main trunk. In fact,

Windows includes a command that lets you view the filesystem as a tree:

TREE

Type that command at the prompt, and you will see your filesystem represented as a tree. It will quickly scroll past your screen – the modern Windows operating system contains many thousands of directories and subdirectories. In the next section, we'll talk about some of the more important directories on your computer's hard drive.

Important Directories

If you go to the root directory of your C drive (or the drive where Windows is installed), you should see a few directories. The most important of the directories is C:\Windows, which contains the system files that make up Windows itself. The Windows directory also contains the C:\Windows\system32 directory, which holds a number of important components and utilities for Windows itself. Do not delete any of the files in this directory! Doing so can disable important parts of Windows, and may even render your system unbootable.

Also in the root directory of your C drive is the C:\Program Files folder. By default, your system's applications install themselves here. If your computer runs a 64-bit version of Windows, you'll also have a C:\Program Files (x86) folder, where Windows installs any 32-bit software programs. All 64-bit applications will go into the regular C:\Program Files folder on a 64-bit Windows system. If you need to uninstall a program, it's a bad idea to simply go into the C:\Program Files directory and start deleting files – you will get better results by uninstalling an application using the Programs and Features item in Control Panel.

The C:\Program Data directory is hidden, but contains a number of application data files and system data files. For instance, all the Start Menu shortcuts are stored in C:\ProgramData\Microsoft\Windows\Start Menu\Programs. Unless you know what you're doing, it's not a good idea to delete or alter files in the C:\Program Data directory.

The root directory of C also holds the C:\Users folder. This folder contains the user profiles – the personal data – of every user who logs into the system. Go into the C:\Users folder, and you will see folders named for every user account on the system. Inside each of those folders, you will see the profile folders for the user – their Desktop folder, which holds the files on their Desktop, their Documents folder, their Pictures folder, and so forth. There are also a number of hidden directories that contain application settings, data files, user preferences, and similar files.

Generally, when working on a computer, it is always a good idea to back up the contents of the C:\Users directory. Especially if it is the personal machine of a technically unskilled user – the user will almost always claim that he or she doesn't "have anything important" on the machine if you need to wipe the hard drive and reinstall Windows. Nevertheless, if you do wipe the machine and reinstall Windows, a few weeks later the user will become irate when he notices that "all his stuff is missing" – and of course the user has no backup copies! It is therefore always a good idea to back up the C:\Users directory when repairing a Windows computer.

3

UNDERSTANDING THE PROMPT

W hen you start the Command Prompt program, the first thing you'll see on your screen is this:
C:\>
That is the actual command prompt itself. But what does the prompt do? What do all those symbols mean? We'll discuss how to understand and alter the prompt in this chapter.

What Is The Prompt?

The "prompt" that gives the Command Prompt its name is the first thing you see when you launch the Command Prompt program. What is it? To put it simply, its a series of characters that indicates the computer is ready to accept commands from you. Nowadays, you know that a computer has booted up and is ready to run programs when you see the Windows desktop. But in the days of DOS, you only knew the computer was ready when you saw the DOS prompt appear on the screen.

The basic prompt in the modern Command Prompt looks something like this:
C:\>

Alternatively, it can have additional directory paths within itself - generally, when you launch a new Command Prompt session, it opens in your home folder, so it will probably look something like this:

C:\Users\USERNAME>

What does this all mean?

If you remember the previous chapter on drive letters, the "C" in the prompt refers to the C drive, your computer's hard drive. You can change the selected drive in Command Prompt by typing the drive letter followed by a colon. For instance, if you wanted to switch from the C drive to the D drive, you would type this and his enter at the prompt:

D:

And then prompt would change from this:

C:\>

To this:

D:\>

If the first letter in the prompt indicates the currently selected drive, the characters after the drive show the current directory and subdirectory on the selected drive. In a prompt that looks like "C:\>", that indicates you are in the root directory of the C drive, since the "\" character represents the root directory of a drive. And as you change the current directory, the prompt changes as well to show the current directory. For instance, if you change from the root directory to the Program Files directory, the prompt will look like this:

C:\Program Files>

As you change into deeper and deeper subdirectories, the prompt will accordingly become longer and longer.

The final character in the prompt, the greater than sign (>), indicates the end of the prompt and the location of the cursor. Any commands you type into the prompt will appear to the right of the greater than sign.

Changing The Prompt

The default prompt configuration is good enough for most people. However, if you would prefer to customize the prompt to show additional (or less) information, you can do so with the PROMPT command. The PROMPT command lets you alter the appearance of the prompt, while customizing it however you wish.

To test it out, type this command at the prompt:

PROMPT Hello!

You'll notice that the command prompt immediately changes from "C:\>" to "Hello!" While having the prompt say "Hello!" seems quite friendly, it nonetheless contains no useful information. To change it back, type this command at the modified prompt:

PROMPT PG

The prompt will then change back to the more familiar "C:\>".

As you might guess, the PROMPT command lets you do more than simply put friendly (or snarky) messages in the command prompt. The PROMPT command responds to a series of variables, and will modify the prompt to display information based on those variables. In the above example, the $P variable refers to the current location, and the $G variable refers to the greater than sign. So when you issue a PROMPT command with the variables in this order, you'll return to the prompt to its default state:

PROMPT PG

Here are some the more useful variables you can use with the PROMPT command to enhance the default command prompt:

-$D adds the current date to the prompt.

-$C adds a left parenthesis.

-$F adds a right parenthesis. You can use this in conjunction with $D to place information provided by the other variables with a set of parentheses.

-$N displays the currently selected drive.

-$P displays both the currently selected drive and the currently selected location on that drive.

-$T shows the current time.

-$V shows the Windows version number.

You can get a complete list of variables for the PROMPT command by using it with the /? switch:

PROMPT /?

(As we mentioned earlier, using the /? switch with any command will provide a list of options for that command. It's a useful switch to remember, in case you can't recall the switches available for any one command.)

Let's combine these variables in a few separate examples. (You can always return to the default prompt with the PROMPT PG command if you make a mistake.) Say you wanted the prompt to show the current date and time along with the drive and location. You would use this command:

PROMPT PGDT

This would alter the prompt to show the current date and time:

C:\>Sun 08/28/201115:08:14.47

However, that prompt looks rather cluttered. It might work better if you put a space between the date and the time with this command:

PROMPT PGSDST

The resultant prompt would look like this:

C:\> Sun 08/28/2011 15:09:17.24

By playing around with the PROMPT command and its variables, you can customize the prompt to your liking.

Changing The Title Bar

By default, the title bar of the Command Prompt window reads simply "Command Prompt." You might want to change it to show more information - if you have multiple Command Prompt windows open, changing the title bar is a quick reminder to let you know what task you are performing in each window. Or you could simply change it for your own amusement.

You can change the text of the title bar with the TITLE command. For instance:

TITLE Hello!

This will change the text of the Command Prompt window from "Command Prompt" to "Hello!"

Changing The Text And Background Color

When you launch a new Command Prompt window, it shows white text on a black background. This a throwback to the old DOS prompt, which always booted up with white text on a black background (or green text on a black background) in order to reduce the chance of the old-style tube monitors burning the text onto the screen. Fortunately, tube monitors have becoming increasingly rare (I don't miss carrying them from building to building) and flat-panel LCD monitors have taken their place.

Reading white text on a black background for a long period of time can put strain on your eyes. If you want to change the color of the Command Prompt's text or background, you can do so with the COLOR command.

The COLOR command generally looks like this:

COLOR 07

If you entered this command at a default Command Prompt window, nothing would happen. Why not? COLOR 07 sets Command Prompt to use white text on a black background. The first digit sets the background color, and the second digit sets the text color. So, COLOR 07 sets Command Prompt to use a black background and white text.

Here is the complete list of codes to use with the COLOR command:

-0, Black.

-1, Blue.

-2, Green.

-3, Aqua.

-4, Red.

-5, Purple.

-6, Yellow.

-7, White.

-8, Gray.

-9, Light Blue.

-A, Light Green.

-B, Light Aqua.

-C, Light Red.

-D, Light Purple.

-E, Light Yellow.

-F, Bright White.

For instance, if you wanted to set the Command Prompt to use white text on a black background, you would use COLOR with these options:

COLOR 70

Or, if you wanted to set Command Prompt to use green text on a black background (to make it look a bit like "The Matrix" science fiction movies), you would use this command:

COLOR 02

Finally, if you make a typo and the Command Prompt is displaying some hideous mixture of colors, like blue text on a black background, simply type the COLOR command without any options. Entering COLOR without any codes after it will reset the prompt back to white text on a black background.

4

WORKING WITH DIRECTORIES

We've already mentioned directories quite a few times in this book. In this chapter, we'll discuss commands for moving from directory to directory, for listing directory contents, creating directories, and deleting directories. With these commands, you will have a thorough knowledge of how to work with directories from the Windows Command Prompt.

Changing Directories

In the previous chapter, we discussed how the prompt changes as you move from directory to directory. But how exactly do you move from directory to directory in the command line? It's not as if you can click on an icon, after all. Fortunately, the command to change the current directory is quick and easy to type - the CD command, which stands for "change directory." For instance, if Command Prompt is in the root (\) directory of C, and you wanted to change to the Users directory, you would type this command:

CD Users

Once you're in the C:\Users directory, if you wanted to move back up to the root directory, you would use this command:

CD ..

Typing the "CD .." command moves you up one directory level. If you're in C:\Windows\system32, the "CD .." command will move you up to C:\Windows. If you're in C:\Windows, "CD .." will move you up to the root directory.

The CD command will let you move to any subdirectories immediately below the level of the current directory. For instance, if you're in the root directory, you need only type "CD Windows" or "CD Users" to change to the Windows directory or the Users directory.

However, CD will not let you jump to a subdirectory two levels down from your current directory. To do that, you'll need to use the full path of the directory to which you want to move. Let's say you are in the root directory of C, and you want to change to C:\Windows\system32. You could type "CD Windows", and then once you're in C:\Windows, "CD system32." However, it might be quicker just to type this:

CD \Windows\system32

With tab completion, it is definitely quicker to use the full path.

Listing Directory Contents

Once you've changed your location to a new directory, the next step is to see the contents of the directory. And you can do that with the DIR command. The DIR command, entered without any switches, displays a list of the files and subdirectories in the current directory. For instance, if you're in the root directory of your C drive, and you type the DIR command, the output will look something like this:

```
07/13/2009 10:20 PM   <DIR>      PerfLogs
   08/16/2011 05:34 PM   <DIR>       Program Files
   08/12/2011 10:13 PM   <DIR>       Program Files (x86)
   03/08/2011 09:44 PM         6,276 shared.log
   08/21/2010 10:43 PM   <DIR>       SIERRA
   04/20/2010 08:00 PM   <DIR>       Users
```

11/07/2007	08:00 AM		5,686	vcredist.bmp
11/07/2007	08:50 AM		1,927,956	VC_RED.cab
11/07/2007	08:53 AM		242,176	VC_RED.MSI
07/30/2011	11:08 PM	<DIR>		Windows

25 File(s)   3,953,909 bytes
6 Dir(s) 811,349,843,968 bytes free

THE DEFAULT OUTPUT of the DIR command produces five columns of information. The first column displays a list of dates - these dates show the last time the file was modified. The second column shows a list of times. This is called a timestamp - it shows the last time the file was modified, and together with the information of the first column, indicates both the date and the time that the file was last changed. The third column is only used if the file listed is in fact a directory - if you see a <DIR> in the line, that means the line belongs to a subdirectory, not a file. The fourth column is only used if the entry actually belongs to a file - the number is the size (in bytes) of the listed file. (To find its size in megabytes, divide the number by 1024.) The final column lists the names of the files and subdirectories in the current directory.

Without any switches, the DIR command only lists the contents if the current directory. If you're in the root directory of C, but you want to list the contents of C:\Windows\system32, you might use the CD command to change the current directory to C:\Windows\system32, and use the DIR command from there. However, the DIR command supports absolute paths:

DIR C:\Windows\system32

Type that command, and DIR will list the contents of the C:\Windows\system32 directory. If you use the absolute path of any directory with the command, DIR will list the contents of that directory, regardless of the directory you currently occupy, if you have proper NTFS permissions to the directory (we'll discuss permissions more in Chapter 5).

As you have seen, the DIR command presents a variety of useful information. Using command switches, you can alter the information DIR displays and view additional data.

The most common switch used with DIR is the /P switch. Let's say you type this command:

DIR C:\Windows\system32

If you do, the results of the command will quickly scroll out of sight. To prevent this, use the command with a slight alteration:

DIR C:\Windows\system32 /P

Instead of scrolling off the top of the Command Prompt window, DIR will instead display the results one screen at a time. Once you've finished examining a screen of information, press any key to scroll to the next screen of information. Keeping pressing keys until you reach the end of the list and return to the prompt. (Alternatively, you can press CTRL-C to cancel the command and return to the prompt.)

The /A switch is another useful option for the DIR command. Type this command in your home directory:

DIR /A

You'll probably see a lot more files than you usually do.

The /A switch does two things. First, it lets you see any hidden files in a particular directory. When a file is "hidden", it has (as you might expect) the hidden attribute set, which means it doesn't show up in Windows Explorer and doesn't appear in the default output for the DIR command. (We'll discuss file attributes more in Chapter 5.)

Second, you can also use the /A switch to look for files that have specific file attributes enabled. For instance, if you wanted to see only hidden files in the current directory, you would use this command:

DIR /AH

To see only files that have the system attribute set:

DIR /AS

To see only files that have the read-only attribute set:

DIR /AR

To see only directories (this switch will list any subdirectories in the current directory, but no files):

DIR /AD

It is possible to mix and match the additional letter after the /A switch. For example, if you wanted to view only directories that were hidden:

DIR /AHD

Another useful option for the DIR command is the /X switch. For the default DIR command, the output looks something like this:

11/07/2007 08:00 AM	17,734	eula.1028.txt
11/07/2007 08:00 AM	17,734	eula.1031.txt
11/07/2007 08:00 AM	10,134	eula.1033.txt
11/07/2007 08:00 AM	17,734	eula.1036.txt
11/07/2007 08:00 AM	17,734	eula.1040.txt
11/07/2007 08:00 AM	118	eula.1041.txt
11/07/2007 08:00 AM	17,734	eula.1042.txt
11/07/2007 08:00 AM	17,734	eula.2052.txt
11/07/2007 08:00 AM	17,734	eula.3082.txt

However, if you were to use the DIR /X command in the same directory, the output would instead look like this:

11/07/2007 08:00 AM	17,734	EULA10~1.TXT	eula.1028.txt
11/07/2007 08:00 AM	17,734	EULA10~2.TXT	eula.1031.txt
11/07/2007 08:00 AM	10,134	EULA10~3.TXT	eula.1033.txt
11/07/2007 08:00 AM	17,734	EULA10~4.TXT	eula.1036.txt
11/07/2007 08:00 AM	17,734	EUD159~1.TXT	eula.1040.txt
11/07/2007 08:00 AM	118	EUFCB1~1.TXT	eula.1041.txt
11/07/2007 08:00 AM	17,734	EU37E0~1.TXT	eula.1042.txt
11/07/2007 08:00 AM	17,734	EULA20~1.TXT	eula.2052.txt
11/07/2007 08:00 AM	17,734	EULA30~1.TXT	eula.3082.txt

You'll notice the extra, trunucated file names before the main filename at the end of the row. As we mentioned in Chapter 1, these are "8.3 filenames", shorter versions of the longer file names used in Windows. You can use the DIR /X command to find these shorter 8.3 filenames.

Why would you need to know these? There are a few situations where knowing the shorter filenames would come in handy. Certain kinds of batch files, for instance, can't handle spaces in file names. Knowing the file's 8.3 name would let you use it in a batch file. Furthermore, some older applications cannot handle long file names, in which case you would need to know the 8.3 filenames in order to use the application.

The DIR command generates quite a lot of information, and you might want to sort it for easier readability. You can do this with the /O switch. By itself, DIR /O doesn't do very much - it simply lists any subdirectories alphabetically, and then any files in alphabetical order. Like DIR /A, the usefulness of DIR /O comes in the additional options you can use with /O.

If you wanted to list files by extension, you would use this command:

DIR /OE

This will list the files by type - all the DOC files (Word documents) would be listed together, all the JPEG files, and so forth.

To list the contents of a directory by size, use this command:

DIR /OS

This will list all the files in the directory, from the smallest to the largest.

If you want to list all the files in the directory by date, use this variant of the DIR /O command:

DIR /OD

This will list the files in the currently directory by age, with the oldest at the first of the list and the newest at the bottom of the list.

DIR /OS will list files by size, from smallest to largest, while DIR /OD will list files by age, from oldest to youngest, but what if you wanted to reverse the order? What if you wanted to list the files from largest to smallest and youngest to oldest? By prefixing a dash (-) to the options of DIR /O, you can reverse the order of the standard listing.

To list files by size, from largest to smallest, use this variant of the DIR command:

DIR /O-S

And to list files by their age, from youngest to oldest, use this variant of the DIR command:

DIR /O-D

Another useful switch with the DIR command is the /Q option.

DIR /Q generates the usual output you've come to expect from the command, but with one additional piece of information – it also lists the owner of the files of the directory. In NTFS file permissions (we'll discuss those more in Chapter 5), the owner of a file generally as full control over it, and can assign permissions to other users on the system or network. Using the DIR /Q command, you can find the owner of files from the command line, which is useful when deciding what NTFS permissions to assign (which we'll also discuss in Chapter 5).

The DIR command, by default, only lists the files in the current directory. By modifying the command with the /S switch, DIR will list the contents of the current directory, as well as the contents of any subdirectories – as well as the contents of any subdirectories within those subdirectories. So as you can imagine, DIR /S command often produces quite a considerable amount of output. In fact, if you use DIR /S in the root directory of your C drive, it will list every single file on your hard drive. Depending upon the speed of your computer and the size of your hard drive, it can sometimes take upward of five minutes to list all the files!

So DIR /S might seem like something of a novelty, but when used in conjunction with the wildcards feature, it is a powerful tool. "Wildcards" are characters that can represent multiple characters, or even all other possible characters. For instance, the question mark character (?) represents one potential character. Let's say you had a series of files in your current directory named Document1.doc, Document2.doc, and so forth up to Document9.doc. To use the question mark wildcard to view just these files, type this command:

DIR Document?.doc

This command will list every single file in the current directory that begins with "Document", has an extension of "doc", and has one additional character before the file extension.

Wildcards are even more useful when you use them with the asterisk (*) wildcard character. The question mark wildcard character only represents a single character. In the example above, the command will list Document1.doc through Document2. doc, but if there's a Document11.doc, the command will miss it, since the question mark wildcard character only represents a single character.

The asterisk, however, represents multiple characters. Let's say you use this command:

DIR *.doc

This command will list every single file with the extension of "doc" in the current directory. Used in combination with wildcard characters, the /S switch suddenly becomes useful. Let's say you wanted to find all the *.doc files on your computer. To do so, you would simply type this command:

DIR *.doc /S

This command will list every single *.doc file on your system. Depending on the size of your hard drive and the number of *.doc files you have, this command might take some time to run. However, you can modify this further with additional combination of wildcards. For example, say you wanted to find every JPEG file on your system that has the word "beach" in the file name:

DIR *beach*.jpeg /S

This command will list every JPEG file on your hard drive that has the word "beach" somewhere in its file name.

The DIR /S command, therefore, can be quite useful for finding files on your hard drive.

Creating Directories

Now that we've discussed how to list the contents of a directory, you might want to create one of your own. To create a directory named "storage", issue this command at the prompt:

MKDIR storage

This will create an empty directory named "storage" in the current directory. Naturally, if you want to create a directory someplace else than the current directory, you'll need to first use the CD command to change your location. Alternatively, the MKDIR command supports using absolute file paths. So if you wanted to create a directory named "temp" in the root directory of your C drive, you would use this command:

MKDIR C:\temp

Note that you can only create directories if you have NTFS permissions of Write or above in the target directory - we'll discuss NTFS permissions in the next chapter.

Removing Directories

From time to time, a directory will outlive its usefulness, and you'll want to remove it. You can remove directories with the RMDIR command. In its default mode, RMDIR only removes directories if they're empty. Let's say you never used the C:\temp directory from the previous example, and you've decided to get rid of it. To remove the directory, use the RMDIR command:

RMDIR C:\temp

This will remove the "temp" directory.

However, if there are in fact files in the directory, you'll receive this error message:

The directory is not empty.

At this point, you have two options. First, you can enter the directory and manually delete any files and subdirectories inside. Or, you could use the RMDIR command with the /S switch to delete the directory, along with any files and subdirectories it contains. To delete C:\temp and any files or subdirectories it holds:

RMDIR /S C:\temp

Be very careful when using RMDIR with the /S switch! If you're not cautious, you can accidentally wipe out large chunks of your files.

5

FILE ATTRIBUTES AND NTFS PERMISSIONS

W e've already mentioned both file attributes and NTFS permissions throughout this book. In this chapter we'll take a closer look at file attributes, and discuss how to view and change attributes from the command line. We'll also examine NTFS permissions, which are considerably more powerful than file attributes, and discuss how to view and alter them as well.

What Are File Attributes?

"File attributes" are basically pieces of metadata that contain additional information about the file. In Windows, files generally have their names, their types (defined by the file's extension), and their timestamps. (Certain kinds of files, such as MP3 music files, have additional kinds of metadata, such as the album and artist name.) With file attributes, however, there are four additional pieces of information that you can add to a file.

These four pieces of information are:

-Archive, represented with the A character. The Archive attribute indicates whether or not a file needs to be backed up – basically, whether or not it has been backed up since the last time the file was altered. The Windows Backup feature makes heavy use of the Archive attribute to determine if a file needs to be backed up or not.

-Hidden, represented with the H character. Hidden files are made invisible to the user – they do not show up in the Windows Explorer window, and are not listed when you use the DIR command. However, we've already explained how to view hidden files with the DIR /A command. Files are generally hidden to protect them from casual deletion – when editing a Microsoft Word document, for example, the temporary files that Word generates are hidden.

-Read-only, represented by the R character. When a file has the Read-only attribute, it cannot be altered. You can open it up and view it, or run it (if it's a program), but you cannot make any changes to do it. Nor can you delete it – if you attempt to delete a file protected by the Read-only attribute, you will receive the "Access is denied" error message.

-System, represented by the S character. Windows uses the System attribute to mark which files are part of the Windows operating system. Needless to say, deleting files marked with the System attribute is a bad idea, since it can result in your computer malfunctioning or even rendering Windows unbootable. For that reason, the System attribute is almost always combined with the Read-only attribute.

Listing File Attributes

How do you find out what attributes a file possesses? You can do that with the ATTRIB command. Enter ATTRIB at the command prompt, and ATTRIB will list every file (including the hidden ones) in the current directory, along with their attributes. The output will look something like this:

```
C:\>ATTRIB
    A       C:\autoexec.bat
    A SHR   C:\bootmgr
```

A SHR   C:\BOOTSECT.BAK
A   C:\config.sys
A SH I C:\hiberfil.sys
A SH   C:\pagefile.sys

(NOTE THAT ATTRIB doesn't generally work with absolute file paths – for most applications of the command, you will have to use it in the current directory.)

As you can see, this is a listing of the root directory of a C drive, and the files' attributes are listed on the left side of the screen, with A for Archive, S for System, H for Hidden, and R for Read-only.

(The I attribute for the C:\hiberfil.sys attribute is a rare one – it simply means a file should not be listed by Windows's built-in indexing for file search. Most regular users, and a good many administrators, will have no need for this attribute.)

Changing File Attributes

You can also use the ATTRIB command to change a file's attributes. For instance, if you wanted to mark the test.txt file as Read-only, you would use this command:

ATTRIB +R test.txt

And if you later changed your mind and wanted to remove the Read-only attribute, you would type this command:

ATTRIB −R test.txt

You can also change more than one attribute at the same time. Let's say you wanted to mark test.txt both as a Hidden file and as a Read-only file. Rather than typing the ATTRIB command twice, you can change both attributes at once:

ATTRIB +R +H test.txt.

And you can also remove both attributes simulatenously:

ATTRIB −R −H test.txt

Using the plus sign (+), the minus sign (-), and the one-letter codes for the four attributes, you can change the attributes on files at your leisure.

The Six Ntfs Permissions

While file attributes are useful, they are obsolete – they're a holdover from the old days of DOS. NTFS file and directory permissions allow you to exercise more powerful and more granular control over individual files. In essence, NTFS permissions allow you to mark a file as Read-only, but only for certain users – other users might have permission to modify and even delete the file. And this is only the beginning of what you can do with NTFS permissions.

First, though, what is NTFS? NTFS stands for "New Technology File System." (A "file system" is a method for organizing the information on a hard disk so the operating system and applications can find it easily.) Microsoft began working on NTFS in the early 1990s as a replacement for the older File Allocation Table (FAT) file system. NTFS has numerous advantages over FAT – it supports larger disk sizes, larger file sizes, is generally faster, and permits you to use NTFS permissions.

But what are NTFS permissions? NTFS permissions are a way of granting specific users specific permissions to files. Let's say that you have two users on a system – Caina Amalas (with a username of camalas) and Lucan Maraeus (with a username of lmaraeus). If you have a file or a directory, you can set different permissions for the two users. You could give camalas full control over the file, while giving lmaraeus permission to only read the file.

There are six major NTFS permissions. Each of the "big six" are composed of many smaller permissions, but for the purposes of most users and administrators, the six major permissions are enough. They are:

-List Folder Contents. This lets a user see the files in a specific directory, but not necessarily open, run, or modify them. To put it simply, a user can use the DIR command to list the files in a directory, but can do nothing with them.

-Read. This lets a user view the contents of a file. Note that if it's a program file, the user cannot run it – he needs the Read & Execute permission for that. Needless to say, the user will not be able to delete and modify any files.

-Read & Execute. This gives the user permission to run an executable file, but not permission to modify or delete it.

-Write. This lets a user both read and make changes to a file. However, the user still cannot delete the file. (Of course, a user could erase all the text or data in the file, leaving the file blank, but he cannot delete the file entirely.) If a directory has the write permission, it allows the user to add files to it.

-Modify. The modify permission allows a user to read, make changes to, run as a program, and delete a file. Basically, the user can do everything to file except change its permissions or change its ownership.

-Full control. The user can do any action to a file – deleting it, modifying it, and changing its ownership and permissions.

You'll notice that the higher permissions are a superset of the preceding permissions. Modify is a combination of Write, Read & Execute, and Read, while Full Control is a combination of the previous five permissions. The full list of the permissions for a file or a directory is called its ACL – its Access Control List.

Listing And Changing Ntfs Permissions

Listing and changing a file's or a directory's NTFS permissions from the Command Prompt uses the same command – the ICACLS command. The ICACLS command is extremely complicated, and has several screens worth of options and command switches – you could write an entire short book about ICACLS on its own. However, here we'll discuss how to use ICACLS to do some basic permission changes.

To find out the NTFS permissions of a file named test.txt, use this command:

ICACLS test.txt

The command should produce output that looks something like this:

TEST.TXT NT AUTHORITY\SYSTEM:(I)(F)
   BUILTIN\Administrators:(I)(F)
   SYSTEMNAME\USERNAME:(I)(F)

THE FIRST LINE shows the name of the file, test.txt. It also shows NT AUTHORITY\SYSTEM, which is one of the groups built into your system. The I in parentheses after the group name means that the file is inheriting its permissions from a parent folder. (In NTFS permissions, "inheritance" means that you can set the permissions on one directory, and then any subdirectories or files created in that directory "inherit" its permissions. Generally, it's a good idea never to disable inheritance unless you have a really good idea, since disabled inheritance can cause all kinds of confusing permissions-related errors.) The F in parentheses means that NT AUTHORITY\System has the Full Control permission for the file.

The next two lines show the groups that have access to the file. The BUILTIN\Administrators group likewise has full control. After that, you'll see a list of users that have access to the file. In this example, SYSTEMNAME\USERNAME is a placeholder for how an entry would look – SYSTEMNAME would be the name of either the local computer or the domain (if the computer is a member of an Active Directory domain) and USERNAME would be the actual username of the user involved.

ICACLS uses one-letter codes to represent the rights as user has to a file.

-N, a user has no access to the file.

-F, a user has full access to the file.

-M, a user has the right to modify the file (this includes the right to delete it).

-RX, a user has the right to read the file and run it as a program, if it's executable.

-R, a user has only read-only access to the file.

-W, write-only access, a user can make changes to the file, but cannot delete it.

-D, a user has the right to delete the file.

You can use ICACLS to change the permissions on a file. For instance, say you wanted to give the user account camalas full control over the test.txt file:

ICACLS text.txt /grant camalas:(F)

This will grant the camalas user account full control over the test.txt file.

Likewise, if you wanted to deny camalas full control over the file, you would use this command:

ICALCS text.txt /deny camalas:(F)

The camalas user account will then be unable to access the test.txt file at all.

An important note – in NTFS permissions, a Deny permission always overrides an Allow permission. For instance, if you were grant camalas the Read permission on test.txt, but also deny the camalas account the Full control permission, camalas would be unable to access test.txt in any way. This can be confusing because user accounts can belong to groups, which have their own permission sets, which can conflict with the individual file's permission.

ICACLS is a complicated command, but you should now know the basics of changing permissions from the Command Prompt.

6

WILDCARDS AND REDIRECTION

W e've already mentioned wildcard characters in this book. However, before we move on to Chapter 7, which will discuss commands for moving, copying, deleting, and renaming files, we should look at wildcards in greater detail. A thorough knowledge of the Command Prompt's wildcard characters will let you issue for more effective commands for manipulating files. We'll also look at "redirection", which lets you feed the output from one command into the input for another.

What Are Wildcard Characters?

Wildcards are characters that represent all possible other characters. As you might remember from Chapter 4, the question mark character (?) can represent every other potential character, and the asterisk (*) can represent any potential combination of characters. Why are wildcards useful? Basically, they let your commands affect more than one file at a time.

Let's say you wanted to use the DEL command to erase a file called test.txt:

DEL test.txt

That command (assuming you had the proper permissions) would delete the test.txt file and do nothing else. But if you add wildcards into the mix, the command can affect multiple files. For instance, add a single question mark to the command:

DEL test?.txt

This command will not delete the test.txt file. It will, however, delete every file in the directory that has "test" in its name, "txt", as its extension, and additional single character before the extension. So test1.txt, test2.txt, and test3.txt, would all be deleted by this single command. Much more efficient than typing DEL over and over again!

However, any of the files that had two characters before the extension – like test10.txt and test11.txt – will not be deleted. This is because the question mark character only serves as a wildcard for a single character. It's useful if you want your command to affect a very narrow subset of files – if you only want to copy a few files, or to delete a few particular files.

To cast a wider net with your command, you need the asterisk (*) wildcard character. The question mark wildcard character represents a single character, but the asterisk wildcard represents any number of characters. For example, consider what would happen if you used an asterisk instead of a question mark with the DEL command:

DEL test*.txt

This command will delete every single file in the current directory that begins with "test" and has an extension of "txt". No matter how many characters come after "test" and before "txt", the DEL command will delete them all.

You can make the DEL command even more powerful by removing the filename and leaving only the asterisk:

DEL *.txt

This command will delete every file in the current directory that has an extension of "txt." We've already mentioned how an asterisk wildcard character can represent any number of characters – here will delete any file, regardless of its name, that has the "txt" extension.

So think about what would happen if you typed this command:

DEL *.*

The use of the asterisk wildcard characters here means that the DEL command will delete any file with any name and any extension. To put it more simply, DEL will delete every single file in the current directory! Needless to say, you should exercise extreme caution while using wildcards with the DEL command.

The wildcard characters work with file manipulation commands other than DEL. You can use the wildcards to make copying and moving files from the Command Prompt far quicker and more efficient.

Redirection

To understand redirection at the Command Prompt, you first to need to understand the ideas of input and output. Input is any information you enter into the computer – a mouse click, or the commands you type at the Command Prompt. Output is information that the computer returns to you – the menu that appears when you right-click the mouse, or the text Command Prompt displays when you enter a command.

Using redirection, you can redirect the output from one command to another command. The most common use of redirection is with the MORE command. If you type the DIR command in a directory that contains a great deal of files, the output will probably scroll off the top of the screen. You could use the DIR /P command to view the output one screen at a time. You have another option with the MORE command and a redirection pipe:

DIR | MORE

The pipe character (|) redirects the output from the DIR command to MORE. The MORE command takes the output and displays it one screen at a time, letting you scroll down line by line. You can also use the pipe character and MORE with the TYPE command. The TYPE command displays the contents of a plain-text file (generally a file with the "txt" extension, though some system INI files are plain-text) on the screen. See this example:

TYPE test.txt | MORE

If test.txt is too long to display on the screen, the MORE command will parse it out one screen of text at a time.

You can also use output redirection create files with the output from the commands. For example, what if you wanted to keep a listing of all the files in a particular directory? You could type the DIR command, of course, but the output would disappear as soon as you closed the Command Prompt window, or even if you typed enough other commands. However, you can avoid the problem if you use DIR with the greater than (>) sign:

DIR > output.txt

When you hit the Enter key, it might seem initially that nothing has happened. However, a new file named "output.txt" has been created in your current directory, and it contains the output from the DIR command. You can display the file with this command:

TYPE output.txt

You can then view the contents of the file.

It is important to take care while using the greater than sign to redirect output. In the previous example, if there's already a file named "output.txt" in the directory, the command will overwrite it, and any data in the original file will be lost. So make sure that you pick a new filename for your output.

However, by using a double greater than sign (>>) you can append the output to an existing file. Rather than overwriting an existing file, the double greater than sign will simply add the output to the end of the existing file. Here's an example:

DIR >> output.txt

You can then read output.txt at your leisure, whether with the TYPE command or with the Notepad application.

Redirecting output to text files might not seem very useful with the DIR command, but it really comes in handy when working with Command Prompt's networking commands. (We'll discuss networking more in Chapter 8.) Many of the networking commands produce long and complicated outputs, and you might want to put the output in a text file to peruse at your leisure.

7

COPYING, MOVING, RENAMING, AND DELETING FILES

I n the previous chapters, we've discussed the basics of the Command Prompt, how to use NTFS permissions, and the basics of managing directories. All the directories in the world won't do you any good if you have nothing to store in them, though. In this chapter we will discuss the basics of managing your files from the command line.

Copying Files

One of the most useful features of the modern PC is the ability to swiftly copy files from one location to another. Practically every computing device has the ability to copy files. The Windows operating system and the Command Prompt are no different. The basic command for copying files from the Command Prompt is the COPY command. If you wanted to use COPY to copy a file called test.txt to the root directory of a USB flash drive assigned the letter J:

COPY test.txt J:

The command will create a copy of test.txt in the root directory of the J drive.

Like most Command Prompt commands, COPY assumes that you

will be copying files from the working directory, and looks there first to find the filenames you specify. However, you can also use COPY with absolute file paths. If test.txt were in the Users directory of the C drive, you would use this command to copy it to J:

COPY C:\Users\test.txt J:

But what happens if there's already a file named "test.txt" in the root directory of J? If there's already a file there, COPY will pause for your confirmation before continuing:

Overwrite J:\test.txt? (Yes/No/All):

If you hit Y to continue, COPY will overwrite the file. Hit N, and COPY will leave the file intact. (The All option is used when copying multiple files at once - hit A, and COPY will not ask you again if you want to overwrite the files for the remainder of the copying job.)

You can override this prompt with the /Y switch:

COPY C:\Users\test.txt J:\ /Y

With the /Y switch, COPY will overwrite any files without first prompting you to continue. Needless to say, you should be careful using the /Y switch, since you might accidentally overwrite valuable data.

Like most other file manipulation commands, COPY works with the wildcard characters. If you wished to copy every file with the "txt" extension in the Users directory to J:\, you would use this command:

COPY C:\Users*.txt J:

The COPY command is easy to use, but it is fairly limited, and has only a few available options. For a more powerful copying utility, Command Prompt offers the XCOPY utility. On the surface, XCOPY works just like COPY - you can copy individual files, use wildcards, and so forth. XCOPY's main advantage over COPY is that it allows you to copy subdirectories. In other words, you can copy entire branches of the directory tree from one location to another with the XCOPY command. In this example, XCOPY will copy the entire contents of your C:\Users directory, including all subdirectories, to the USB drive at J:

XCOPY C:\Users*.* J:\ /S /E

You will notice the use of two switches, /S and /E. The /S switch tells XCOPY to copy all the subdirectories in the C:\Users directory. The /E switch tells XCOPY to copy the subdirectories even if they are empty.

Here are a few more useful switches XCOPY offers:

-/M copies only files with the Archive attribute enabled, and then switches it off. This essentially lets you use XCOPY as a crude backup utility.

-/D:m-d-y only copies files changed after the specified date (for instance, for December 27th, 2010, the command would look like this: **XCOPY *.* /D:12-27-2010**).

-/C tells XCOPY to continue the copy operation even if there are errors. This is useful when copying large numbers of files from a failing or damaged disk - if you're trying to copy off, say, 85 gigabytes worth of music files, it is quite irritating to have the operation fail two gigabytes into the job due to an error.

-/H tells XCOPY to copy files with the System and Hidden attributes, as well.

-/R overwrites any files with the Read-only attribute in the destination directory that share same name as the copied files. You should be careful with this option, since it can cause data loss.

-/N copies the files using their 8.3 filenames.

-/Y works the same as the /Y switch with the COPY command, and tells XCOPY to overwrite any files of the same name without prompting you first.

The COPY command is good enough for quickly copying small groups of files, but for heavy-duty file copying, you'll want to use the XCOPY command.

Moving Files

There are two ways to move a file. You could copy the file to its new destination, and then delete the original source file. This involves unnecessary work. Using the MOVE command, you can move a file from its original location to a new one, all in a single command. If you wanted to move the test.txt file to a USB flash drive at J:

MOVE test.txt J:

This will move test.txt to the root directory of J, while removing the original source file.

Like COPY and XCOPY, the MOVE command supports the use of wildcard characters. This command will move every file in the current directory to the root directory of J:

MOVE *.* J:

Renaming Files

Very often you will need to change the name of a file or of a directory. Renaming a file is quite simple, thanks to the REN command. In the following example, you use the REN command to change the name of test.txt to example.txt:

REN test.txt example.txt

Likewise, you can also use the REN command to change the name of directories. For instance, if you wanted to change the name of the C:\test directory to C:\finished, you would use this command:

REN C:\test C:\finished

The REN command has a few caveats, though. The renamed file has to stay in the same location as it started - you cannot use the REN command like the MOVE command, in other words. In addition, you cannot rename a file to match the name of a file that already exists in the current directory - you cannot use REN like the COPY or the XCOPY commands to overwrite a file.

Deleting Files

Deleting files from Windows Explorer is simple enough - you simply drag and drop them to the Recycle Bin icon on your desktop. This works well enough for one or two files, but becomes quite cumbersome if you want to delete, say, one hundred files at once. Especially if the files are mixed with other files that you want to keep - you'll need to cumbersomely scroll down while CTRL-clicking the files, or drag them one by one to the Recycle Bin.

Either way is a waste of time, especially when you can delete files quickly and easily from the Command Prompt.

The command to delete files (and directories - we'll discuss that later) is the DEL command. If you wanted to delete a file named test.txt in the current directory, you would use this command:

DEL test.txt

The test.txt file will be deleted in short order.

If, however, the file has the Read-only attribute, you'll get an error message that says "Access is denied." If this happens, you have two options. You can use the ATTRIB command to revoke its Read-only status and then delete the file. Alternatively, you can use the DEL command with the /F switch:

DEL /F test.txt

The /F switch tells DEL to delete the file, even if it has the Read-only attribute. You should of course take considerable care when using the /F switch, since you might inadvertently delete important files.

If you don't have NTFS permissions to the file, you can't delete it. You'll need to first alter the permissions so you have at least the Modify permission, or log onto your Windows system using an account (such as administrator account) that has the permissions.

Like XCOPY and COPY, the DEL command also works with the wildcard characters. Using DEL with the wildcard characters makes the command extremely powerful (and extremely dangerous). For example, if you have a series of files named data1.doc, data2.doc, and so forth, you could delete them all at once using the question mark wildcard character:

DEL data?.doc

This will delete every file in the current directory hat begins with data, has an extension of "doc", and has a single character after the "data" part of the filename. (It works much like the previous example with the COPY command, except instead of copying the files, DEL deletes them.)

Using the asterisk wildcard character with DEL creates an even more powerful command:

DEL *.doc

This command will delete every single file with the "doc" extension in the current directory. If you use it conjunction with the /F switch, it will wipe out files with the Read-only attribute.

If you remember what we've discussed about the asterisk wildcard character, then you know what this command will do:

DEL *.*

This will delete every single file in the current directory. Needless to say, you should only use this command when you are absolutely certain that you want to delete every single one of the files in the current directory.

Like XCOPY, the DEL command isn't confined to working in a single directory at a time. This command will tell DEL to delete every file with the "doc" extension in the current directory, and every file with the "doc" extension in the current directory's subdirectories:

DEL *.doc /s

And to take it one step further, this command will delete all the files in the current directory, and all files in all the current directory's subdirectories as well:

DEL *.* /s

Needless to say, you should exercise great caution when using this command.

Like XCOPY and COPY, DEL also works with absolute file paths. For instance, if you wanted to delete every file in the C:\temp directory, you would employ this command:

DEL C:\temp*.*

Using DEL, you can delete files from the Command Prompt more efficiently than through Windows Explorer. Just use it carefully - you can accidentally wipe out important data.

8

NETWORKING

The Windows Command Prompt is based off the old DOS command line, and DOS had hardly any networking commands. Back in the days of DOS, computer networking was still in its infancy, and therefore DOS had no need of networking commands. Stand-alone workstations were more common than computers joined together in local area networks.

All that has changed. Nowadays, a computer is far more likely to be connected to some kind of network (whether a home connection or workplace LAN) than not. In fact, computers that are not connected to the Internet in some form are increasingly rare. This means that Command Prompt has numerous commands dealing with networks, networking, and IP addresses, and we'll discuss those commands in this chapter.

What Is An Ip Address?

First, however, we should discuss IP addresses. Before we explain the Windows Command Prompt's networking commands, it's a good idea to have a firm grasp of the basics of IP addressing.

The letters "IP" stand for Internet Protocol, and the Internet

Protocol is part of the TCP/IP (Transmission Control Protocol/Internet Protocol) suite, a group of related protocols that lay down the rules for how computers communicate over networks, both over LANs and the larger Internet. An IP address, therefore, is a (theoretically) unique address assigned to a computer. It's a bit like a street address - it lets other computers send traffic to and receive traffic from your system. An IP address consists of four groups of numbers separated by dots:

192.168.1.1

These numbers are actually the numerical form of a binary number. None of these numbers can be higher than 255. (While watching a detective TV show, it's occasionally hilarious to see the police track a criminal using a ludicrously implausible IP address, like 689.34.385.339.)

The dominant version of the IP protocol is Version 4, commonly referred to as IPv4. Under IPv4, there are only 4.6 billion IP addresses available, and the available IP addresses ran out a few months before the time of this writing. (IPv6, which has many more available addresses, will eventually replace IPv4, but for now, IPv4 remains dominant.) There are obviously far more computers, phones, routers, switches, and other networked devices in the world than 4.6 billion, so how do all these devices receive IP addresses?

The answer is a "private IP address." Certain blocks of IP addresses have been reserved for use in private networks. These blocks, using a technology called Network Address Translation (NAT), are then "translated" to public IP addresses. This has extended the lifetime of the available IPv4 address space for decades. The ranges of the reserved private addresses are:

10.0.0.0 - 10.255.255.255

172.16.0.0 - 172.31.255.255

192.168.0.0 - 192.168.255.255

Odds are, your computer has an IP address in one of those ranges as part of a private network (even if it's just a private network generated by your wireless router).

IP address also have a "subnet mask". A subnet mask defines

which parts of the IP address designate the network, and which part designates the individual computer. Let's say the IP address of 192.168.1.1 from above has a subnet mask like this:

255.255.255.0

That means the 192.168.1 part of the address indicates the network, while the final 1 indicates the computer.

IP addresses usually include a "broadcast" address. Any traffic sent to the broadcast address is directed to every single computer in the local network. A broadcast address has a "255" as its final number, so a computer with a 192.168.1.1 address will have a broadcast address of 192.168.1.255.

Lastly, IP addresses usually (but not always) come with a "default gateway". The default gateway is the address you computer sends traffic destined for anywhere outside the local network segment. Like, say you want to visit Google with your web browser. Your computer recognizes that Google isn't on the 192.168.1.* network, and so forwards the request to the default gateway, which then sends the traffic on to Google. (This is a simplification, but adequate for our purposes.)

Finding Your Ip Address

Find your IP address from the Command Prompt is quite easy, and in fact (as we mentioned in the Introduction) quite a bit easier than doing it from the GUI. Simply go to the Command Prompt and type this command:

IPCONFIG

The IPCONFIG command stands for "IP Configuration", and in its default state it spits out quite a bit of information about your computer's network configuration. The most important information is found under two different headings. You can find the information for your computer's Ethernet adapter under the heading marked "Ethernet adapter Local Area Connection." (If you have more than one Ethernet adapter, each additional adapter will be labeled Local Area Connection 2, Local Area Connection 3, and so forth.) If your computer has a wireless network card, as most laptops do, it will have a heading marked "Wireless LAN adapter Wireless Network Connection."

The important information will look like this:

IPv4 Address. . . . . : 10.10.8.100

Subnet Mask . . . . : 255.255.255.0

Default Gateway . . . . :10.10.8.200

Here you see listed your computer's IP (version 4) address, your subnet mask, and your default gateway.

There is a second command available to find your IP address. It takes longer to type, but it presents much less extraneous information than IPCONFIG. The Command Prompt includes a command called NETSH (for "net shell") to perform network tasks from the command line, and you can use it to find your IP address:

NETSH INTERFACE IPV4 SHOW ADDRESS

The command's output will look something like this:

Configuration for interface "Wireless Network Connection"

DHCP enabled:	**Yes**
IP Address:	**10.10.8.100**
Subnet Prefix:	**10.10.8.0/24 (mask 255.255.255.0)**
Default Gateway:	**10.10.8.200**
Gateway Metric:	**0**
InterfaceMetric:	**25**

Using either IPCONFIG or NETSH INTERFACE IPV4 SHOW ADDRESS will allow you to view your IP address from the command line.

Finding The Mac Address And Other Information

Finding your IP address is useful, but there are other pieces of networking information that you might need. Your computer's DNS server, for one – DNS stands for "Domain Name Service", and a DNS server translates easy domain names, like http://www.jonathan-moeller.com, into appropriate IP addresses. You might also need to find your computer's MAC address. MAC stands for "Media Access

Control", and every network adapter has its own unique MAC address burned into the hardware. (Theoretically, anyway – it's relatively simple to fake a MAC address.)

IPCONFIG in its default state does not show the MAC address. But like every other command, it includes switches. With the /ALL switch, IPCONFIG shows a great deal more information:

IPCONFIG /ALL

Here's some of the information the command will list for each network adapter on your system:

Connection-specific DNS Suffix . :
Description . . . . :
Physical Address. . . . . :
DHCP Enabled. . . . . :
Autoconfiguration Enabled . . . . :
Link-local IPv6 Address . . . . . :
IPv4 Address. . . . . :
Subnet Mask . . . . :
Lease Obtained. . . . . :
Lease Expires . . . . :
Default Gateway . . . . :

DHCP SERVER . . . . :
DHCPv6 IAID . . . . :
DHCPv6 Client DUID. . . . . . . :

DNS SERVERS . . . . :

PRIMARY WINS SERVER . . . . :
NetBIOS over Tcpip. . . . . . . :

Your computer's MAC address will be listed under the "Physical Address" item. You can also find the address of your DNS servers under the "DNS Servers" item.

There is a quicker way to find your MAC address with the GETMAC command. Type this command, and it will list the MAC address for every single network adapter on your system:

GETMAC

However, the default output generated by the GETMAC command is not terribly useful. It lists the adapters by "transport name", which is generally a long string of letters and numbers. It's quite difficult to figure out which transport name corresponds to which adapter. Fortunately, using the /V switch with GETMAC produces a more informative ouput:

GETMAC /V

This sorts the output by the name of the connection (Local Area Connection, etc.) and therefore makes it much easier to find which MAC address goes with which adapter.

Renewing And Releasing Ip Addresses

There are two ways to give a computer an IP address, static and dynamic. With a static IP address, you manually assign an IP address to a computer, and it never changes. This works well enough for small networks, but on a network with hundreds or even thousands of computers, keeping track of which computer has which IP address quickly becomes overwhelming.

The second method is a technology called DHCP, which stands for Dynamic Host Configuration Protocol. With DHCP, the network administrator configures a DHCP server for the network. When a computer connects to the network, it communicates with the server and receives an IP address. With the IP address comes a "lease", the amount of time the computer gets to keep the address. Usually, the computer renews its lease with the DHCP server halfway before the time expires.

DHCP is automated, and the process is supposed to be invisible to the user. Like any technical process, things sometimes do go wrong. A common one is that the computer has an expired IP address, yet refuses to release it (this often happens when you move a computer to a different network with a different DHCP server). You can use the IPCONFIG command at the Command Prompt to force your computer to release any DHCP address. Type IPCONFIG with this switch:

IPCONFIG /RELEASE

This will release your computer's IP addresses.

(Note that you must be running Command Prompt as an administrator for this command to work.)

You can also use IPCONFIG to contact the network's DHCP server for a new address. Generally, when you connect your computer to a new network, it should automatically contact the DHCP server to receive an address. But if you've just released the address, your computer might not re-contact the DHCP server. You can force it to renew the lease on its IP address with this command:

IPCONFIG /RENEW

If your computer doesn't have a DHCP-assigned address, it will attempt to contact a DHCP server and get an address. If your computer already has an address, it will contact the DHCP server and renew its lease on that address.

Setting A Static Ip Address

Under most circumstances, most computers do not need a static IP address (especially if there's a DHCP server on the network). Most server systems, however, need a static IP. Server software likes stability, and is liable to malfunction every time the server receives a new DHCP IP address. For that matter, keeping a static IP makes it easier for client systems to find the target server.

You can set a static IP address using the NETSH command. If you wanted to set a static IP address on the "Local Area Connection" Ethernet adapter of 192.168.1.100, with a subnet mask of 255.255.255.0 and a default gateway of 192.168.1.200:

NETSH INTERFACE IPV4 SET ADDRESS "LOCAL AREA CONNECTION" STATIC 192.168.1.100 255.255.255.0 192.168.1.200

Note that you need to run NETSH from the Command Prompt as an administrator.

Having a static IP address will not do you much good unless you also set the address for the DNS sever. Most DHCP servers supply the address of a DNS server as part of the address information, but if you use a static address, you'll need to set it on your own. Fortunately, you can do this with NETSH. If you wanted to set a DNS server address of 192.168.1.200, you would use this command:

NETSH INTERFACE IPV4 SET DNSSERVERS "LOCAL AREA CONNECTION" STATIC 192.168.1.100

These two command will let you first set a static IP, and then assign a DNS server address to your computer.

If you change your mind and want to use a DHCP address again, you can also set your computer to use a DHCP address from the Command Prompt. To set your computer to receive a dynamic IP address on the "Local Area Connection" adapter, use the NETSH command:

NETSH INTERFACE IPV4 SET ADDRESS NAME="LOCAL AREA CONNECTION" SOURCE=DHCP

To tell your computer to receive its DNS server address from the DHCP server, use this version of the NETSH command:

NETSH INTERFACE IPV4 SET DNSSERVERS NAME="LOCAL AREA CONNECTION" SOURCE=DHCP

This will configure your computer to receive a DNS server address from the DHCP server.

Diagnosing Network Problems

If you've ever had to repair a computer (or even used one, for that matter), you know that network and Internet connection problems are a depressingly common occurance. And you also know that Windows's built-in graphical tools for solving network problems are not often that useful. Fortunately, the command line's tools are much better at getting practical information.

The first and most commonly used network-diagnostic command

is the PING command. PING stands for "Packet Internet Groper", and it relies upon the ICMP protocol, the Internet Control Message Protocol. Basically, the PING command sends a packet to a network destination, such as a server or another PC, and if the destination is activate, it sends back an acknowledgement packet. For instance, if you wanted to ping the PC at the IP address of 192.168.1.2, you would use this command:

PING 192.168.1.2

If 192.168.1.2 is up, the PING command will generate an output like this:

Reply from 192.168.1.2: bytes=32 time=1ms TTL=127

Reply from 192.168.1.2: bytes=32 time=1ms TTL=127

Reply from 192.168.1.2: bytes=32 time=1ms TTL=127

Reply from 192.168.1.2: bytes=32 time=32ms TTL=127

PING also has a few command options you can use to alter its performance. The /T switch tells PING to continuously send packets until you use CTRL-C to tell it to stop:

PING /T 192.168.1.2

This is useful to continuously test a connection, since it will allow you to see if it is intermittently dropping traffic.

You can also use the /N switch to tell PING to send a certain number of packets. In this example, PING will send six packets, and then stop:

PING /N 6 192.168.1.2

Note that the PING command will not always work, even if a remote destination has an active network connection. This is because Windows 7, by default, blocks ICMP traffic, and several other operating systems do the same. However, enough devices do permit ICMP traffic to make PING a useful diagnostic tool.

Tracing Paths

Sometimes your network connection is active, but you can't access a particular destination. In this case, the TRACERT command becomes useful. TRACERT maps the network route from your computer to the destination, and sends every device in the path an ICMP packet. You can then see which devices in the path are not responding, and then hopefully determine a solution. For instance, to trace the path to 192.168.1.2, you would use TRACERT like this:

TRACERT 192.168.1.2

The output will look something like this, with one line for each "hop" (another device in the chain) to the destination:

1   1 ms   1 ms   1 ms 10.10.11.254

2   54 ms   1 ms   1 ms 192.168.1.2

TRACERT, by default, runs up to thirty hops, but you can use the /H switch to force a higher or lower number of hops.

Dns Problems

DNS is a bit like the circulatory system in the human body. When it's working right, you will forget that it's there. But when it goes bad, everything grinds to a halt. DNS is much the same way. Without it, you can't type addresses into the addresses bar of your web browser, or use any network resources that depend upon DNS.

You can use the NSLOOKUP utility to determine if your DNS server is functioning or not. NSLOOKUP runs a query against the DNS server, and if the server is active, the command produces a response. Specifically, it looks up the IP address of the domain name you used with the command. For example, this is what the command to look up the IP address of Google.com would look like:

NSLOOKUP google.com

The command would generate an output like this:

Non-authoritative answer:

Name: google.com

Addresses: 74.125.225.84

74.125.225.83

74.125.225.81

74.125.225.82

74.125.225.80

If NSLOOKUP does not generate a response, you know that

either your DNS server is having problems, or your computer cannot communicate with the DNS server due to a connection problem.

Tracking Network Statistics

The Command Prompt also includes a powerful utility for tracking network statistics – the NETSTAT command. Issuing the NETSTAT command without any switches at the command line displays a list of currently active network connections to your computer. NETSTAT comes with a variety of switches that improve its usefulness:

-/A, which lists all connections and open ports on your computer.

-/E, displays the Ethernet statistics – how many bytes of data your computer has sent and received, and so forth.

-/S, displays the statistics on a per-protocol basis – TCP, IP, ICMP, and others.

NETSTAT is a fairly advanced utility, but you can use it to help track down obscure network problems afflicting your computer.

9

DISK MANAGEMENT

Most users don't think about disk management – they turn on their computers, plug in their flash drives, and expect everything to simply work. However, if you want to install a second internal hard drive in your computer, you'll need to partition and format it. Or you might need to repartition and reformat an external USB hard drive, or (for really advanced users) a USB flash drive.

You can accomplish all these tasks via the Disk Management snap-in in the Microsoft Computer Management graphical application. However, you can just easily do so from the command line. The Command Prompt includes a powerful utility called DISKPART that allows you to manage disks, partitions, and volumes from the command line.

In this chapter we'll show you the basics of using DISKPART.

Two Caveats

Before we start using DISKPART, there are two points you should keep in mind.

First, DISKPART has to be run as an administrator. You'll need to run DISKPART in a Command Prompt window with administrative rights (we discussed how to do that in Chapter 1). If you try to run DISKPART without administrative rights, you'll only receive the usual "Access is denied" error message.

Second, DISKPART is a powerful utility. With a few keystrokes, you can wipe out entire hard drive partitions - and all the data contained on those partitions. Needless to say, you should take extreme caution while using DISKPART, lest you accidentally destroy large quantities of critical data.

With those points in mind, let's discuss the DISKPART prompt.

The Diskpart Prompt

DISKPART is different from the other commands we've discussed in this book. For most of these commands, you type the command and its options at the prompt, and view the output after the command finishes processing. DISKPART, however, has its own prompt. When you type the DISKPART command, the familiar C:\> prompt will change to the DISKPART prompt, which will look like this:

DISKPART>

The normal commands will not work in DISKPART. You will need to use special DISKPART commands, which we will discuss later in this chapter. To leave the DISKPART prompt and return to the normal Command Prompt window, simply type EXIT.

Disks, Partitions, Volumes

DISKPART works with disks, partitions, and volumes. But what do these terms mean?

A "disk", in DISKPART parlance, refers to the actual physical disks themselves. Your hard drive is a disk. So are any USB flash drives, USB hard drives, or optical disks.

A "volume" is a bit more nebulous and harder to define. A "volume", in Windows, describes a mounted storage device represented by a drive letter. Your C: drive is a volume by this definition. The actual physical disk itself is a "disk" in DISKPART, but the logical filesystem on the disk, along with the drive letter, counts as a volume.

A "partition" in DISKPART is a virtual division on a disk. You could, if you chose, divide a hard drive into four separate virtual parts, and each one of those pieces would count as a partition. Note that a partition is not the same thing as a volume. A volume is formatted with a file system (usually NTFS, but sometimes FAT or FAT32) and has been assigned a drive letter by Windows. A partition is simply a logical division of a physical disk – the partition might be empty, and might not even have been formatted with a file system.

Every volume, however, is placed within a partition. Your hard drive has a partition – most computer hard drives have one big partition that fills the primary hard drive. (Consumer laptop and desktop hard drives generally have one big partition, and a smaller "system restore" partition that contains the Windows reinstallation files in case the computer's operating system becomes corrupt or virus infected.) To sum up the terms – a physical disk can be divided into partitions, and the partitions can be formatted and mounted as volumes.

Listing Disks, Partitons, And Volumes

DISKPART's commands are context-specific. That means before using a command to alter a disk, a partition, or a volume, you have to first select the volume from the DISKPART prompt. (Needless to say, this makes selecting the proper disk, partition, or volume extremely important!)

But before you can select the appropriate disk, volume, or partition, you need to first employ the LIST command. Using the LIST command, you can find out what disks, volumes, and partitions are on your system. More importantly, you can find out what numbers Windows has assigned those items, since you'll need to know the numbers in order to select them. So, to find out all the disks on your system, you would use this command from the DISKPART prompt:

LIST DISK

The output will look something like this:

Disk ### Status   Size   Free   Dyn Gpt

-------- ------------- ------- ------- --- ---

* Disk 0   Online   149 GB   0 B

Disk 1   Online   1959 MB   0 B

In this example, the computer has two disks, Disk 0 and Disk 1. (Computers, using binary, start counting from 0 instead of 1.) Disk 0 is a 149 gigabyte hard drive, while Disk 1 is a two gigabyte (approximately) USB flash drive. Why does Disk 0 have an asterisk character (*) in front of it? That means that Disk 0 is the currently selected disk – any DISKPART commands that affect a disk will affect Disk 0.

To see all the current volumes on your system, use this command:

LIST VOLUME

The output will look something like this:

Volume ### Ltr Label   Fs   Type   Size   Status   Info

---------- --- ----------- ----- ---------- ------- --------- --------

Volume 0   D   DVD-ROM   0 B No Media

* Volume 1   C   NTFS Partition   148 GB Healthy

System

Volume 2   E   FAT Removable 1959 MB Healthy

In this example, the computer has three volumes, Volumes 0, 1, and 2. The output also shows the volume's drive letter in the "Ltr" column, its filesystem in the "Fs" column, the kind of volume (DVD-ROM, Removable disk, etc.) in the "Type", and the size in gigabytes or megabytes in the "Size" column. In this example, Volume 1 is selected – hence the asterisk before its entry in the output. Any commands that affect volumes will affect Volume 1 (in this case, the computer's C drive).

To find the partitions on the currently selected disk, use this command:

LIST PARTITION

The LIST PARTITION command will generate an output like this:

Partition ### Type   Size   Offset

------------- ---------------- ------- -------

* Partition 1   Primary   1959 MB   31 KB

Remember, the LIST PARTITION command only lists the partitions on the currently selected disk, not the partitions on every single disk attached to the system. In this example, we are looking at the single partition on the USB flash drive from the earlier examples. As before, Partition 1 (the only partition on the flash drive) is selected, and therefore has the asterisk in front of it.

Selecting Disks, Partitions, And Volumes

Listing disks, partitions, and volumes is well and good, but you'll still need to select them, since using a DISKPART command on the wrong target can prove disastrous. You can select targets of your choosing using the SELECT command. To use the SELECT command, first use the LIST command to view the disks, volumes, or partitions currently available. Make note of the number assigned to each object. For instance, if you wanted to select disk 1, you would use this command:

SELECT DISK 1

This will select disk 1. If you use the LIST DISK command afterward, you will see that disk 1 is now the current disk. Selecting volumes works much the same way. If you wanted to SELECT volume 1, use this command:

SELECT VOLUME 1

If you run the LIST VOLUME command after this, you will see that Volume 1 is now the selected volume.

Selecting partitions works a little differently. To select a partition, you must first use SELECT DISK to select the disk you want to use, and then LIST PARTITION to see the available partitions on the disk. To then select Partition 0 on the disk, you would use this command:

SELECT PARTITION 0

If you then use LIST PARTITION, you will see that Partition 0 is now the selected partition.

Remember that you can only select partitions after you have first selected the disk containing the partition.

Cleaning Disks

Once you've selected a disk, you can then issue commands that will affect that disk.

The most drastic command you can use is the CLEAN command. The CLEAN command completely clears off a disk – all volumes and partitions on the disk are deleted. Generally, it's best to use CLEAN when preparing a new disk, or wiping an old one. Make sure you've selected the right disk before using CLEAN – it is quite possible to wipe out valuable data with a single mistyped command!

(Note that the CLEAN command does not overwrite the deleted data – it is still there, and can be removed. To securely wipe a hard drive, you'll need to find a third-party utility that does secure disk erasure.)

Creating Partitions

Once you have a blank disk, you can use DISKPART to create partitions on it. You could do that with DISKPART'S CREATE command. You can create five kinds of partitions using CREATE PARTITION, but for this book we will focus on three of them – a primary partition, the extended partition, and the logical partition.

Every disk can have only one primary partition. If a disk has only one partition, it's almost always one big primary partition filling up the drive. Windows's key boot files (like boot.ini and ntldr.exe) must be located on a primary partition in order for the system to boot up.

Likewise, each disk can only have one extended partition. The extended partition is essentially a secondary partition – people will sometimes partition their hard drives so that the system files are located on one partition, and their data files on the second. However, some hard drives have more than two partitions on the disk. How is this accomplished? The answer is logical partitions – each extended partition can contain a larger number of logical partitions. So, if you wanted to divide your hard disk into five separate volumes, you could create a primary partition, an extended partition, and then create the remaining number of logical partitions inside the extended partition.

To create a partition on a disk, first select it with the SELECT command. Then, use the CREATE command to create a partition of the type and size you want. For instance, to create a primary partition:

CREATE PARTITION PRIMARY

This command will create a partition that fills up the entire disk. If you want to limit the size, use CREATE with the SIZE modifier. For instance, this command will create a primary partition of 20 gigabytes on the currently selected disk:

CREATE PARTITION PRIMARY SIZE=20000

Note that the SIZE modifier uses megabytes for its measurement, and there are (approximately) 1000 megabytes in a single gigabyte. So if you wanted a partition of 20 gigabytes, you would tell the CREATE command to create a partition with a size of 20000 megabytes.

To create an extended partition, use this command:

CREATE PARTITION EXTENDED

As with a primary partition, you can also use SIZE to specify the size in megabytes of the desired partition.

To create a logical partition, you'll need to first select an extended partition using the SELECT PARTITION command. Once you've selected the logical partition, use this command to create the logical partition:

CREATE PARTITION LOGICAL

As with the previous two examples, you can use the SIZE modifier to limit the space the newly created logical partition will use. This is useful if you want to put more than one logical partition within the extended partition.

Creating Volumes

After you've create partitions, you can create volumes upon your partitions. DISKPART lets you create several different kinds of volumes, including RAID partitions, but for the purposes of this demonstration we'll stick to creating simple volumes. To create a simple volume, use this command:

CREATE VOLUME SIMPLE

You can also use the SIZE modifier to regulate the size of the simple volume. For instance, to create a simple volume with a size of 20 gigabytes:

CREATE VOLUME SIMPLE SIZE=20000

As before, the size is measured in megabytes.

Formatting Volumes

To "format" a disk means to prepare it with a filesystem for use with your computer. A disk (usually) doesn't come with a filesystem prein-stalled - it's simply a blank slate. Formatting the disk with a filesystem marks the disk with a storage system, which means your computer can then read and write data to the disk.

In DISKPART, you format volumes, not disks or partitions. To format a volume, first select it with the SELECT command, and then use the FORMAT command. The FORMAT command comes with a few options to alter its performance. The most commonly used one is the FS options, which lets you specify which filesystem to use with the volume. For instance, to format the volume with the NTFS filesystem:

FORMAT FS=NTFS

You can also select the FAT or FAT32 filesystems. Why would you use a different filesystem than NTFS? Generally, any internal hard disks on your computer should be formatted with NTFS (and any partition where Windows is installed has to be formatted NTFS). Using NTFS on your internal hard disks let you make use of NTFS permissions to secure your files. If you have a USB flash drive, however, it's often best to format it with FAT or FAT32. Mac OS X and Linux computers generally can read from, but not write to, NTFS volumes, and if your flash drive is formatted NTFS Mac and Linux systems will not be able to write data to it. (Of course, for certain secure implementations, you may want to format your USB flash drive with NTFS.)

Assigning Drive Letters

Once you've created volumes and formatted them, you can use DISKPART to assign the volumes drive letters. You can do this with the ASSIGN command. To use it, select the volume you that will receive a letter. Once you've selected the appropriate volume, use this command to assign it (for example) the drive letter H:

ASSIGN LETTER=H

This will assign the drive letter H to the selected volume.

You can use this command to change the letter of already created volumes - just select the appropriate volume with the SELECT command and then use the ASSIGN command to change the letter. However, take care when doing this, since you might accidentally alter file paths that a program needs to use - Windows Backup, for instance, might become annoyed that the path of your backup hard drive has changed from E:\ to F:\.

Note that you cannot change the drive letter of the volume containing the Windows pagefile. In most cases, the pagefile is located on the same volume as the Windows system files.

Deleting Partitions

Deleting partitions from DISKPART is easy. It is so easy, in fact, that you should exercise extreme caution while doing so, lest you accidentally destroy important data in the process. You can delete partitions using the DELETE PARTITION command. If you wanted to delete Partition 1 on Disk 0, first select Disk 0, and then Partition 1, using the SELECT command. Once the appropriate partition on the correct disk has been selected, use the DELETE PARTITION command:

DELETE PARTITION

This will delete Partition 1 on the currently selected disk. If the partition is an extended partition, any logical partitions within it will be deleted as well.

Note that you must first select the correct disk before deleting any partitions upon it. It's best to be very careful about this - if you accidentally delete Partition 1 on Disk 1 instead of Partition 1 on Disk 0, you run the risk of destroying important data.

Deleting Volumes

Deleting volumes is somewhat less destructive than deleting partitions, and runs less risk of accidentally wiping out large chunks of data (provided, of course, you choose the correct volume). To delete a volume, first select the volume you want to delete with the SELECT command, and then use the DELETE VOLUME command:

DELETE VOLUME

This will delete the selected volume.

As always, take care when deleting volumes, and double-check that you have selected the correct volume before deleting it.

10

CONNECTING TO FILE SHARES

As we mentioned in Chapter 8, the Windows Command Prompt is based off the old DOS command line, and DOS had barely any networking commands. Starting with Windows for Workgroups, Windows focused heavily on networking, and also on file sharing. "File sharing" is one of the most basic functions of computer networking. It basically means making files available to other users and systems via a network connection. Shared folders are generally referred to as "file shares" or more simply as "shares." Microsoft has for years made it easy to share files from Windows (maybe too easy, given how quickly viruses spread over the Internet in the first years of the 21st century).

But do you need to use Windows's graphical tools to access file shares? Not at all! DOS might have lacked file-sharing commands, but the Windows Command Prompt includes them. Using these commands, you can connect and disconnect from shared folders, and even create your own shares.

Mapping Network Drives

You might have heard people talk about "mapping a network drive." What does that phrase mean? "Mapping a network drive" refers to taking a shared network folder it and making it appear on your Windows system with a drive letter. When you plug in a USB flash drive or a USB hard drive, you're used to it appearing in the Computer window with the next available drive letter. By mapping a network drive, you can make it appear in Computer with a drive letter, just like any other external drive. You can then issue commands from the Command Prompt to move, delete, and copy files to and from the network share.

Assuming, of course, that you have the proper share permissions, which we shall discuss in the next section.

Share Permissions

We've already discussed NTFS permissions in Chapter 5. Share permissions, however, are something entirely different from NTFS permissions. NTFS generally deal with which users and groups can access a file. Share permissions control which users can access the shared folder or file, and what level of access they have to the folder, over a network connection. However, NTFS permissions can override share permissions. If you have the share permission to add files to a shared folder, but your account only possesses the NTFS Read permission, you will not be able to copy any files to the share.

This can seem confusing, but taken piece by piece, share permissions are straightforward. In fact, there are six major NTFS permissions, but only three share permissions: Read, Change, and Full.

The Read share permission gives a user permission to view the file or folder over the network. It works a lot like the Read NTFS permission. A user with the Read permission will be able to see the file in the directory, open up the file, and read it. However, the user will not be able to alter the file or delete it.

The Change share permission gives the user permission to alter a shared file. Basically, it functions like the NTFS Write permission. The user has permission to change a file with the Write permission, but he cannot delete the file, and he cannot change its share permissions.

The Full share permission, like the NTFS Full Control permission, gives the user complete control over the file or folder. If you have the Full share permission, you can read the file, make changes to it, and delete it. You can also alter its share permissions for other users.

What happens when the share permissions and NTFS permissions conflict? The rule of thumb is that the most restrictive permission wins. For instance, say you have the Full share permission to a file, but only the NTFS Read permission. You'll be able to read the file, but the NTFS permissions will block you from editing the file in anyway. Likewise, let's say you have the NTFS Full Control permission for a file, but only the Read share permission. You'll be able to read the file, but since your share permissions are limited to Read, you won't be able to do anything else with it.

Viewing File Shares

The first step to connecting to file shares from the Command Prompt is to find those shared folders. To connect to a file server, you'll need to know either its IP address, or its Fully Qualified Domain Name. (A FQDN is a computer's proper DNS name - for instance, fileserver.test-domain.com.) Whether connecting via the IP address or the FQDN, you'll need to use a syntax called UNC - Uniform Naming Convention. UNC is a technology Microsoft uses in Windows to designate the location of a network resource. For example, if you have a file server at 192.168.1.1 which contains a shared folder named Data, the UNC path to the server and the folder would look like this:

\\192.168.1.1\data

You'll need to use UNC to designate the server and folder you want to use when working with file shares from the Command Prompt. Let's say you want to view the shared folders available on a server with the IP address of 192.168.1.1. To do so, you would use the NET command. The NET command is the Swiss army knife of the Command Prompt. It does a variety of different things, and is your chief tool for connecting to file shares from the command line. More specifically, you would use the NET VIEW command to view the available file shares on a server:

NET VIEW \\192.168.1.1

The command will generate an output that should look something like this:

Shared resources at \\192.168.1.1

Share name Type Used as Comment

----

images   Disk

data   Disk

backup   Disk

The command completed successfully.

From this output, you can see that the server at \\192.168.1.1 has three separate shared folders available - images, data, and disk. You can then use this information to connect to the file share and map it as a network drive, which we'll discuss how to do in the next section.

Connecting To A File Share

To connect to a file share, you again use the NET command. To connect, however, you'll use the NET USE command, rather than NET VIEW. If you wanted to connect to the data fileshare on \\192.168.1.1 and map it as your computer's H drive, you would use this command:

NET USE H: \\192.168.1.1\data

This will mount the shared folder "data" at \\192.168.1.1 as your computer's H drive.

Unfortunately, if you reboot your computer, or log out and then log back into your account, this will break your connection to the share, and you'll have to remap the network drive all over again. You can avoid this by using NET USE with the /PERSISTENT switch:

NET USE H: \\192.168.1.1\data /PERSISTENT:YES

This will tell Windows to remap the network drive every time you log into your account. If the network share is available when you log in, Windows will remap the drive for you.

You might also need to connect to the share as a different user. This can be accomplished via the /USER switch with the NET USE command. If you wanted to connect to the \\192.168.1.1\data share using the user account named camalas, you would use the NET USE command with these parameters:

NET USE H: \\192.168.1.1\data /USER:CAMALAS

This will connect you to the network share at \\192.168.1.1\data using camalas's user account.

Disconnecting From A File Share

If you no longer need a particular network drive, you might want to disconnect it. Just as with mapping a network drive, you can disconnect a network drive from the Command Prompt via the NET USE command. To disconnect the H drive we mapped in the earlier example, you would use this command:

NET USE H: \\192.168.1.1\data /DELETE

Using the /DELETE switch might seem rather drastic. Fortunately, the /DELETE switch is misnamed. It doesn't delete any of the files or subdirectories contained in the file share. It only disconnects the mapped network drive from your computer, and you can reconnect to it at your leisure.

Create A File Share

In addition to connecting to file shares from the Command Prompt, you can also create your own file shares using the command line. Windows Vista and Windows 7 are generally called "client systems", since they're designed to interact with larger server systems running a version of Windows Server. However, the client versions of Windows can act as limited server systems. You can created shared folders on your Windows client system, and allow users to connect to them remotely.

As with finding and connecting to network shares, you use the NET command to create file shares on your Windows computer. To create network shares, you use the NET SHARE version of the NET command. Let's say you have a directory named data in the root directory of your C drive you want to share. To make it into a shared folder, use this command:

NET SHARE DATA=C:\DATA

This will set C:\DATA as a shared folder with a share name of "DATA." The new share won't do you very much good unless you assign share permissions to users. You also use the NET SHARE command to assign share permissions to users. For instance, if you wanted to grant the camalas user account the Read permission to the DATA share:

NET SHARE DATA /GRANT:CAMALAS READ

This will assign the camalas user account the Read share permission. To assign the Change permission to the camalas user account, use this command:

NET SHARE DATA /GRANT:CAMALAS CHANGE

And to grant the Full share permission:

NET SHARE DATA /GRANT:CAMALAS FULL

Finally, to view all the file shares on your system, use the NET SHARE command without any arguments:

NET SHARE

This will generate a similar output to using NET VIEW to view the file shares on a remote system, but this listing will show only the file shares on the local system.

11

MANAGING USER ACCOUNTS

T o use a Windows computer, you need a user account on that computer. Most home computers generally have one local account with administrative rights, and the user never gives it another thought. Windows computers that are part of a large business network are usually members of an Active Directory domain, with their user accounts stored on one of the domain's controllers. Active Directory is beyond the scope of this book, but in this chapter, we'll show you how to create and manage local accounts from the Command Prompt.

What Is A User Account?

Before we begin, you should have a clear idea of what a user account is, and the difference between local user accounts and Active Directory user accounts.

To put it simply, a "user account" is a set of credentials that allow a user to log into a Windows computer system. "Credentials", in this context, is the term that computer security experts use to describe the pieces of information a user must present in order to access the computer. Most of the time, the credentials consist of two pieces of information - your username, and your password. However, you can have additional credentials, as well - more secure computer systems might require you to present a username, a password, and a smart card, or a USB flash drive with an encryption key stored upon it. Advanced systems can even require biometric credentials - your fingerprints, for instance. The vast majority of home computers are not so secure, and usually require only a username and a password (and some home computers are configured not even to require a password, which is always a bad idea).

There are two kinds of user accounts you will encounter in a Windows system - local user accounts, and Active Directory domain user accounts. Local user accounts are stored on one specific Windows computer, and work only on that particular Windows system. If you have a computer named System1, and a user account called camalas on that computer, then the camalas account will only work on System1. If you tried to use the camalas user account on another computer named System2, it would not work. You could set up an identically named local account on that computer named camalas, but it would not be the same account. Local accounts work fine for individual computers, or for computers on smaller networks, but managing local user accounts on a large network of hundreds or thousands of computers quickly becomes impractical.

This where Active Directory user accounts come in. In Active Directory, individual Windows computers are joined to the Active Directory domain. Each Active Directory domain controller stores a database of user accounts, and a user can log into any domain computer using his Active Directory account. The local accounts still exist on the domain member computers - most organizations leave a local administrator account in case of technical trouble, and perhaps a restricted local account for guest users.

In this chapter we'll focus on managing local accounts from the Command Prompt.

Finding User Accounts

The first step managing local user accounts is to know what accounts you actually have on your system. As with managing file shares, you can accomplish this with the NET command. This time, we'll be using the NET USER variation of the NET command. To find out the names of all the local accounts on your Windows system, issue the NET USER command without any arguments or switches:

NET USER

The output should look something like this:

User accounts for \\SYSTEMNAME

Administrator　　　Guest　　　　　camalas
The command completed successfully.

In this example, NET USER is listing all the local accounts for the \\SYSTEMANME Windows system. You can see that the computer has three accounts - the built-in Administrator account (which is disabled by default in Windows Vista and Windows 7), the built-in Guest account (also disabled by default), and the camalas account.

Displaying Information About A Specific User Account

NET USER without any options lists the accounts on a system, but provides no other information about them. To get specific information about an individual local account, use the NET USER command with the name of the account. For instance, to find out specific information about the camalas account, use this command:

NET USER CAMALAS

If the account name has a space in it (as local accounts on a home computer often do), you'll need to enclose the account name in quotation marks:

NET USER "CAINA AMALAS"

Regardless of the account name, the output should look like this:

User name　　　　　Caina Amalas
Full Name

Comment
User's comment
Country code   000 (System Default)
Account active   Yes
Account expires   Never
Password last set   4/20/2010 8:00:30 PM
Password expires   Never
Password changeable   4/20/2010 8:00:30 PM
Password required   No
User may change password   Yes
Workstations allowed   All
Logon script
User profile
Home directory
Last logon   9/10/2011 12:32:42 PM
Logon hours allowed   All
Local Group Memberships   *Administrators   *Debugger Users
Global Group memberships   *None

There's quite a bit of information here, but we'll go over the more important bits.

"User name", obviously, is the actual user name, the name of the account. "Full name" is often blank, but it's sometimes used if the username is a truncated version of the user's full name - a username of "camalas" with a full name of "Caina Amalas", for example. "Account active" indicates whether or not the account is disabled, and "account expires" indicates when the account is going to expire - user accounts can be configured to expire on a certain date (for a temporary employee, for instance).

The section of information dealing with the password is important. It shows when the password was last set, when it expires, and whether or not the user can change his password. It is possible to set a password policy forcing users to change their passwords after a set period of time. You can see the date of the password's expiration in NET USER's output, as well.

"Last logon", as the name indicates, shows the last time the user account logged into the computer. "Logon hours allowed" displays the hours when the account can log into the computer. This is useful if you want to restrict the times a user can use his account - a work employee can log in only during business hours. Or if you have children, you can restrict the hours they can use the family computer.

Finally, the "Local Group Memberships" field shows the local groups to which the user account belongs. If you want a user to have administrative rights, the account needs to be a member of the Administrators user group.

Adding A User Account

NET USER can be used to view information about accounts already on your Windows system, but you can also employ it to add additional accounts. The basic format is to use NET USER with the /ADD switch and the account name. So to add a user account named camalas to your system, you would use this command:

NET USER CAMALAS /ADD

This command will add a user account of camalas to your computer. Note that an account name can only have a maximum of twenty characters.

However, you can also use NET USER and /ADD in conjunction with other command switches. You can also set the password associated with the camalas account right away through the use of the /PASSWORDREQ switch. To set camalas's account with a password of Cymr!Yy29 (note that passwords, unlike the rest of Command Prompt, are case senstive):

NET USER CAMALAS Cymr!Yy29 /ADD /PASSWORDREQ:YES

You can also set a full name for the account right away by using the /FULLNAME switch:

NET USER CAMALAS /ADD /FULLNAME:"Caina Amalas"

Restricing User Accounts

Now that you know how to add user accounts, you may need to restrict the times that users can log into the system. You can do this by using NET USER with the /TIME switch. For example, to set that camalas account so that it can only log into the system on Mondays through Fridays from 6AM to 6PM:

NET USER CAMALAS /TIME:M-F, 06:00-18:00

This will restrict camalas from using the computer from 6 AM until 6 PM on Mondays through Fridays.

Disabling User Accounts

You might find it necessary from time to time to disable a user account. Usually, this happens when an employee is fired unexpectedly, and you need to lock his account to prevent him from accessing sensitive information. Or, if you are a parent, and your child misbehaves, you can punish him by locking his account on the family computer. Disabling a user account deactivates it without deleting it entirely - the account is still there, but locked, and cannot be used to access the computer. To lock the camalas user account from the command line, use this command:

NET USER CAMALAS /ACTIVE:NO

This will disable the camalas user account. To reactivate it, use the same command, but change the /ACTIVE switch from NO to YES:

NET USER CAMALAS /ACTIVE:YES

This will reactivate the account.

Deleting User Accounts

Disabling user accounts is a useful ability, but if you have no further need of an account, there's no reason to keep it on your computer.

Furthermore, an unused account represents a security risk - if an attacker were to guess the password, he would have access the account. And if the compromised account is an administrative account, he would have complete access to all of your computer's files and settings.

It is generally best to disable accounts rather than delete them entirely - there's always a chance you might need the account in the future, after all, and disabling an account is almost as secure as deleting it entirely. However, if you're absolutely certain you have no further need of an account, you can delete it using the NET USER command with the /DELETE switch. To delete the camalas account from our previous examples, you would use this command:

NET USERS CAMALAS /DELETE

This will delete the camalas user account. Note that the account is gone forever - if you need to bring it back, you will have to create a new account with the same name.

12

REMOTE ACCESS

For several years, Mac OS X and Linux systems have had a significant advantage over Windows systems. Using a technology called SSH (SSH stands for Secure Shell), Mac OS X and Linux system administrators could remotely log into their systems via the command line. Once logged in, they could control their remote systems through the command line, operating the computer as if they were sitting in front of it.

Windows, of course, has had remote access technology for years, via the Remote Desktop or Terminal Services software. Using Remote Desktop, you could remotely log into a server computer, seeing an entire graphical desktop on your computer. This is useful, but Remote Desktop has a few disadvantages over the text-based SSH – it's often quite slower, and on a slow connection with a lot of latency, Remote Desktop can become sluggish. And as with all GUIs, Remote Desktop is less efficient than the command line. To perform a task on a remote computer, you would have to fire up the Remote Desktop client, log in, and then execute the task via the mouse. Using SSH, it's far quicker to execute tasks on a remote Mac OS X or Linux machine – you merely log in using the SSH shell, type the command, and the task is finished. Windows lacked a software feature that could perform a similar remote management function.

All this changed with the introduction of WinRM – Windows Remote Management.

What Is Winrm?

WinRM stands for Windows Remote Management. It is a Microsoft implementation of the SOAP protocol that lets you manage and control remote Windows machines over a network connection. The "SOAP" in the SOAP protocol stands for Simple Object Access Protocol, a set of rules for exchanging information over an HTTP web connection. One weakness of SSH is that it runs over specific TCP/IP ports (traditionally port 22, though most SSH server software lets you change the port), and that specific ports needs to be unblocked to allow SSH connections. SOAP runs over HTTP, and many firewalls allow HTTP traffic. Therefore, it's possible to run WinRM without opening up any additional firewall ports.

WinRM runs on Windows XP, Windows Vista, Windows 7, Windows Server 2003, Windows Server 2003 R2, Windows Server 2008, and Windows Server 2008 R2. (Though you'll need to install some patches from Microsoft in order to use WinRM on Windows XP.) WinRM has some substantial limitations, but it is quite useful, and hopefully Microsoft will improve it with future versions of Windows.

In the next section we'll walk you through doing a basic setup of WinRM.

Enabling Winrm

Performing a basic setup of WinRM is extremely easy, and takes only one command. First, launch a Command Prompt as an administrator (the setup will not work if you run the Command Prompt as a normal user). After the Command Prompt window launches, type this command:

WINRM QUICKCONFIG

After you type this command, it will ask if you want to proceed. Hit Y to proceed, and WinRM will activate itself (though you may need to reboot before it functions). What exactly does this command do?

First, it starts the WinRM service, and sets it to delayed automatic start (this means the service will start automatically when your computer boots, but only after other, more important services have first launched). Second, it configures Windows to accept commands from remote computers, even commands that require administrative rights. Third, it tells the WinRM listener to accept requests from the HTTP port. Finally, it opens a firewall exception in the local Windows firewall, so that the HTTP traffic can actually reach the WinRM listener.

Now that WinRM is enabled, you can use it to launch commands from a remote computer.

Using Winrs

To actually send commands to a computer running WinRM, you need to use the WINRS command. WINRS is short for "Windows Remote Shell", and allows you to send command from your local Command Prompt to a remote computer running WinRM. Note that you must have an administrative account (or a domain account with administrative rights) on the target computer for WINRS to execute your command.

In this example, we'll assume you want to send remote commands to a computer named System1, and that the computer is a member of the Fake.com domain. The DIR command is a good one to test with WINRS. This command will produce a listing of the root directory of the C drive on System1:

WINRS –R:SYSTEM1.FAKE.COM DIR C:

Let's go through the options in this command step-by-step.

WINRS, of course, launches the WINRS shell for sending commands to a remote system. The -R switch tells WINRS which computer should receive the command. The -R switch is followed by the colon (:) character, and immediately after the colon is the name of the computer that should receive the command. For the basic set up of WinRM, you'll need to use the FQDN (fully qualified domain name) of the remote computer to receive the command. Finally, after the FQDN comes the command to send to the remote computer.

You can launch any command you want via WINRS, with one important exception. The command cannot require any user input. Basically, if a command needs user input - like if it asks you to press Y to continue or N to cancel - it will not work. This does limit what you can do with WINRS, but with careful planning, you can avoid the limitations. (Like by using /Y switch with the XCOPY and COPY commands to keep them from asking for confirmation when over-writing a file.) However, some commands, like DISKPART, simply cannot be used via WINRS.

Using Winrs As A Different User

Sometimes, you may need to run a remote command as a different user than your current account. WINRS also gives you this ability. To run a command as a different user, use the -U switch with WINRS. For instance, if you wanted to view the root directory of the C drive on System1 using the camalas account, you would use the WINRS command with this syntax:

WINRS -R:SYSTEM1.FAKE.COM -U:CAMALAS DIR C:

WINRS will ask you for camalas's password. Assuming you enter the password (and assuming that camalas has administrative rights on the target system), the command will list the files in the root directory of System1's C drive.

13

BATCH FILES

As you have probably realized by now, while using the Command Prompt is in many circumstances more efficient than using the GUI, it nonetheless involves a great deal of repetitive typing. However, there are way to automate commands, and the easiest way to automate commands from the Command Prompt is to use a batch file. With a batch file, you can launch a dozen commands (or more) in sequence simply by typing the name of a single file from the command line.

In this chapter we'll discuss how to use a simple batch file.

What Is A Batch File?

To put it simply, a batch file is a text file containing a sequence of commands, one in each line. When you launch the batch file from the command line, Command Prompt reads the file, executing each of the commands in sequence. (That means Command Prompt first executes the command on the first line, then the second, then the third, and so on until it reaches the end of the file.)

Using a batch file, you can automate tedious jobs, or tasks that require typing several command in sequence. For instance, let's say you have a daily task on your Windows computer that requires you to enter twelve commands in sequence to complete it. You could type out each command one by one, with the attending risk of making a typing error. Or you could put the commands into a batch file named JOB.BAT, and run it from the command line. Command Prompt will execute each of the commands in sequence, and you needn't worry about any typographical errors.

Creating Batch Files

How do you create a batch file?

Any text editor (an application that saves files as plain text files) will work to create batch files. The most popular application for creating batch files is the Microsoft Notepad utility included with Windows. Notepad has been included with every version of Windows since version 1.0 was released in 1985. (Which, I suspect, makes Notepad older than many of the readers of this book!) Notepad is very bare bones, but it will make a clean text file for you to use as a batch file. You'll need to make sure you save it as a BAT file instead of a TXT file - go to the File menu, and then to Save As, change the "Save As Type" to "All Files", and type the file name with a BAT extension.

It's a bad idea to use a full-featured word processor like Microsoft Office Word or LibreOffice Writer to create your batch file. The standard save formats of full-featured word processors are obviously not text files, and even when saving a Word document as a TXT file, it tends to be formatted incorrectly. If you want a more full-featured text editor, there are several free programs available - Notepad++ is one of the more popular ones.

Unfortunately, Windows does not include a text editor you can use from the Command Prompt. It's possible to create text files from the Command Prompt by using the ECHO command and output redirection, but even then, there's no way to edit the file once it has been created. This is one area where Mac OS X and numerous Linux distributions have the advantage over the Windows Command

Prompt, since they include the vi text editor, which lets you edit text files from the command line (assuming you master vi's syntax and commands, of course).

Batch Commands

You can put practically any command in a batch file. There are, however, a set of ten commands that are particularly useful for adding functionality to batch files (and some of them only work properly when used in a batch file). Using them, you can create limited programs that accept user input, complete with assigned variables. These will be simple programs - to create really complex effects, you'd need to learn WMI (Windows Management Instrumentation) syntax or a programming language like C# or Visual Basic. Nevertheless, you can use these commands to create useful batch files.

The ten batch file commands are ECHO, CALL, FOR, PAUSE, CHOICE, GOTO, REM, IF, SHIFT, SET. Some of them are beyond the scope of this book, but we'll take a look at the simpler ones in this chapter.

Echo

The ECHO command does just what its name indicates - it "echoes" back a line of text. Entered from the command line, the command will "echo" back whatever text follows the command. For instance, this command would generate an output of "HELLO!"

ECHO HELLO!

The ECHO command has two uses in creating batch files. First, you can use it to display directions on the screen, or an explanation of what the batch file is doing. Second, you can use it to generate cleaner output from your batch files. By default, the batch file displays every command on the screen, along with its output. However, prefixing any command with a @ symbol prevents it from appearing on the screen. And if you use the @ symbol with the

ECHO OFF command, it makes the prompt disappear for the dura-
tion of the batch file:

@ECHO OFF

This is useful if you don't want your batch file to clutter up the
screen while it runs.

Pause

The PAUSE command does exactly what its name says. It pauses
processing of the batch file until you press a key to continue. Issuing
the PAUSE command from the Command Prompt generates this
output:

Press any key to continue...

The Command Prompt will wait until you press a key to return
control to the prompt. When inserted into a batch file, PAUSE stops
the execution of the file, which is useful when you want to view some
output before it scrolls off the top of the screen.

Rem

The REM command doesn't actually do anything.

Despite that, it is quite useful. REM stands for "remark", and
when used in a batch file, the Command Prompt will ignore any text
that comes after it. This is handy for inserting "remarks", or notes,
into your batch file. Why would you want to do that? The REM
command allows you to document your batch files. If you write a
batch file and need to edit it a year later (because, say, some server
names or IP addresses changed) you might look at some of the
commands and wonder why you put them in there. REM lets you
make notes as you write the batch file, so you can examine them later
and remember why you put the file together the way that you did.

The second use of the REM command is for testing. Using REM,
you can "comment out" a command by prefixing REM before it. The
Command Prompt will then treat the command as a remark and
ignore it. This comes in handy when you are testing a batch file that

does not work properly, allowing you to pin down which part of it isn't working as you thought.

Goto

The GOTO command tells the Command Prompt to jump to a new location in the batch file. If you programmed old BASIC or Microsoft QBASIC programs, you might remember using GOTO statements with the numbered lines of code. GOTO in the modern Command Prompt works a bit different. GOTO jumps to a text line designated by a colon character (:) and resumes processing the commands in order. For instance, consider a GOTO command that looks like this in your batch file:

GOTO :SELECT

If you have a command like this, GOTO will jump to the line in the batch file beginning with :SELECT.

Choice

The CHOICE command does exactly what its name implies - it presents you with a choice. Typing the CHOICE command at the prompt generates an output that looks like this:

[Y, N]?

This looks rather similar to other Yes or No choices offered by other Command Prompt commands. By itself, CHOICE does nothing. You need to use it in conjunction with other commands (particularly the SET command) in order to make it useful. However, you can alter the appearance of the CHOICE command with a few convenient command switches. The /M switch lets you add a custom message to the CHOICE command (with the message itself in quotation marks). This command is generates a message of "Hello! Press Y or N":

CHOICE /M "Hello! Press Y or N"

If you want to have different options than to press Y or N, you can modify the options with the /C switch. This command prompts the user to press 1, 2, or 3, rather than Y or N:

CHOICE /C 123

You can also use the CHOICE command with a default option, and set it to choose that default option after a timeout measured in seconds. This version of the CHOICE command sets the default option to Y, after waiting 90 seconds for user input:

CHOICE /D Y /T 90

Using these switches, you can customize the choice offered by CHOICE to fit your needs.

Set

The SET command is a powerful tool that ties together the GOTO and CHOICE commands, allowing you to offer real choices in your batch files. By itself, the SET command primarily works with "environment variables." Environment variables are a number of system variables with preset values that control the way both the Command Prompt and Windows itself work. To see the environment variables for your system, use the SET command from the prompt without any switches:

SET

This generates quite a long list of output - Windows uses numerous environment variables. To quickly find the value for any one variable, you can use the ECHO command. However, you need to use the ECHO command with special characters. The TIME variable displays the system time, so you might be tempted to use this command:

ECHO TIME

However, this will only display the word "TIME" on the screen. To use ECHO to display system variables, you'll need to enclose the variable within a pair of percentage characters (%), like this:

ECHO %TIME%

This time, rather than just spitting out "TIME", the output will look like this:

22:13:30.56

You can also use the SET variable to create your own environment variables. To create a variable entitled "TODAY" with a value of "Wednesday", use this command:

SET TODAY=Wednesday

Then if you use that variable with ECHO, it will return with a value of "Wednesday":

ECHO %TODAY%

Assign your own variables might seem like a pointless game, but it becomes useful when working with your own batch files. Using the SET command, you can create a batch file that will execute instructions based on the user's choices. With the /P switch, you can instruct SET to create a new variable based upon the user's input - in effect, the /P switch combines CHOICE and SET into a single command. Let's say you wanted to create a variable named INPUT, and offer the user a choice between Option 1 and Option 2. The SET command to create such a choice would look something like this:

SET /P INPUT="Press 1 for Option 1, and Press 2 for Option 2: 1,2: "

Combined with the GOTO and the IF commands, this lets you create batch files that offer choices. (Note that the message text has to be in quotation marks, and the actual option keys themselves need to be enclosed in colon characters, as shown in the example.)

If

The IF command ties together batch processing. The IF command responds to the variable created by the SET command. For every potential value of the previously created variable, you can then tell the IF command to perform a specific task. Generally, the best use of the IF command is to issue the GOTO command, which will then route Command Prompt to the section of the batch file containing the necessary commands.

This example shows the best use of the commands we've explored in this chapter. This batch file offers the user a choice between pressing "C" for a listing of the root directory of the C drive and "D" for a listing of the root directory of the D drive. Depending upon which choice the user takes, he is moved to a different portion of the batch file, which then executes the necessary commands:

```
@echo off
set /p input="Press C for C:\, and press D for D: C,D: "
if %input%==1 goto C
if %input%==2 goto D
:C
dir C:\
goto end
:D
dir D:\
goto end
:end
```

By following this example, you can create your own batch files using variables and choices.

14

TASK MANAGEMENT

I f you've used Windows for any length of time, then you've probably encountered the Task Manager – the graphical utility that lets you observe system performance, see which applications and processes are running on your system, and manually kill processes that become unreliable or freeze up. There are several commands that let you perform many of the Task Manager's functions from the command line. In this chapter, we'll show you how to manage processes from the command prompt. Using the commands in this chapter, you'll be able to list running processes on your computer, and terminate ones that become troublesome.

What Is A Process?

In Windows, a "process" doesn't refer to the specific procedure you use to do something, or a standardized method for carrying out a task. Rather, a process is defined as the active instance of a computer program. For example, if you ran the Firefox web browser, Firefox would be a running process. Once you exit Firefox and close your browsing session, the process would exit and disappear.

A process can also be a background program running on your

computer, either a background program you installed yourself or a component of Windows. If you launch Task Manager (or use the commands described later in this chapter) you will see dozens of processes. Most of them will be background components of Windows itself, like the print spooler or the networking services.

Generally, Windows handles its processes, whether applications or built-in Windows services, pretty well, and you don't need to think about them. But like anything else, there can be problems. Sometimes a process will freeze up and refuse to quit, and you will need to forcibly terminate it. Additionally, some processes can seize so much of your computer's available memory or CPU power that your system slows to a crawl and becomes nonresponsive. If that happens, you'll need to find out which process is hogging the resources and terminate it.

In the next section, we'll show you how to list currently running processes on your computer.

Listing Running Processes

To view the running processes on your computer, use this command:

TASKLIST

This will immediately list every running process on your Windows computer. This will probably scroll off the screen, so you might want to pipe the output to the more command to let you view the output one screen at a time:

TASKLIST | MORE

By default, tasklist lists five different pieces of information about the processes running on your system. The first, Image Name, is basically a friendly name that allows you to find the process quickly in a list. The second, PID, stands for Process Identifier. Windows assigns a Process Identifier number to every process on your system, and the PID turns up in several log files.

The third piece of information, Session Name, identifies whether or not a process is a Services session or a Console session. Basically, a Services process is one launched by Windows to run in the background, while a Console process was launched by the user logged into the computer. On a Windows Server system, you can also see RDP under Session Name – that means a user logged onto the server via Remote Desktop Services launched the process.

The fourth piece of information is Session Number, listed as Session#. On a client Windows system, you'll generally only see two numbers – 0 for processes launched by Windows, and 2 for processes launched by the logged-in user. On a Windows Server system running Remote Desktop, you will often see more numbers.

The final piece of information, Mem Usage, simply lists the amount of memory a specific process is using.

You can get even more information from the tasklist command if you use it with the /v option:

TASKLIST /V

When used with the /v command, TASKLIST provides four additional columns of information. The first, Status, displays what the process is currently doing. Most of the time, this will say Running, but if a process has frozen up, it could say Not Responding. Processes launched by Windows will say Unknown, since Windows has control of them.

The second piece of information is User Name, which lists the user that launched the process. Usually, this will be the user currently logged into the system. If you are using this command on a Remote Desktop Services system, this can help you track down which user launched which process, which is very useful if a specific process is hogging all the system resources.

The third piece of additional information is CPU Time, which shows how much CPU time each process has used. As with Mem Usage, this can help you track down a process that is using too many system resources. The final piece of information is Window Title. If a process has also opened a window on the desktop, the title of the window is listed here. If you have an errant application that refuses to close and you do not know the name of its process, you can help use the title of its window to find its process here.

Terminating Processes

Generally, when processes work, you don't have to think about them. If you are going to the trouble of listing processes, that probably means one or more processes have malfunctioned and you need to forcibly shut them down. Listing processes allows you to find which processes you need to terminate. To terminate a process from the Command Prompt, use this command:

TASKKILL

By itself, taskkill only spits on an error message. To make proper use of it, you need to specify either the image name or the PID of the process you wish to terminate. For instance, if you wanted to terminate a process with an image name of application.exe, you would use TASKKILL with the /IM switch to specify the image name:

TASKKILL /IM APPLICATION.EXE

This would kill the APPLICATION.EXE process immediately.

You can also use the /PID switch to specify TASKKILL to terminate a process with a specific PID. To return to our previous example, if APPLICATION.EXE has a PID of 1234, you can use this command to terminate it by PID:

TASKKILL /PID 1234

Additionally, the TASKKILL command offers two additional switches you can use with either the /PID switch or the /IM switch. First, the /F switch forcibly terminates the process, which is useful if you have a recalcitrant process that simply refuses to terminate. Second, the /T switch also terminates any child processes that the process launch. So, if you wanted to terminate a process with a PID of 1954, while also forcing it to terminate and terminating any child processes, the command would look like this:

TASKKILL /T /F /PID 1954

The process would then be terminated, along with any child processes.

AFTERWORD

I hope this book has been a useful introduction to the Windows Command Prompt.

Windows - and the entire technology world - changes very rapidly. Since this is an ebook, I hope to update it regularly to reflect the changes made to Windows in particular and computing technology in general.

ABOUT THE AUTHOR

Standing over six feet tall, Jonathan Moeller has the piercing blue eyes of a Conan of Cimmeria, the bronze-colored hair a Visigothic warrior-king, and the stern visage of a captain of men, none of which are useful in his career as a computer repairman, alas.

He has written the DEMONSOULED series of sword-and-sorcery novels, and continues to write THE GHOSTS sequence about assassin and spy Caina Amalas, the COMPUTER BEGINNER'S GUIDE series of computer books, and numerous other works.

Visit his website at:

http://www.jonathanmoeller.com

Visit his technology blog at:

http://www.computerbeginnersguides.com

Made in the USA
Las Vegas, NV
22 October 2020